America's Asian Alliances

The BCSIA Studies in International Security book series is edited at the Belfer Center for Science and International Affairs at Harvard University's John F. Kennedy School of Government and published by The MIT Press. The series publishes books on contemporary issues in international security policy, as well as their conceptual and historical foundations. Topics of particular interest to the series include the spread of weapons of mass destruction, internal conflict, the international effects of democracy and democratization, and U.S. defense policy.

A complete list of BCSIA Studies appears at the back of this volume.

America's Asian Alliances

Robert D. Blackwill and
Paul Dibb
Editors

BCSIA Studies in International Security

The MIT Press
Cambridge, Massachusetts
London, England

Library of Congress Cataloging-in-Publication Data

America's Asian alliances / Robert D. Blackwill and Paul Dibb, editors.
p.   cm.—(BCSIA studies in international security)
Includes bibliographical references.
ISBN 0-262-02489-6 (hc. : alk. paper)—ISBN 0-262-52285-3 (pbk. : alk. paper)
1. Asia—Foreign relations—United States. 2. United States—Foreign relations—
Asia. 3. United States—Foreign relations—1993– . I. Blackwill, Robert D.
II. Dibb, Paul. III. Series.
DS33.4.U6 A64   2000
327.7305—dc21   00-025896

2 4 6 8 10 9 7 5 3 1
Printed in the United States of America

Contents

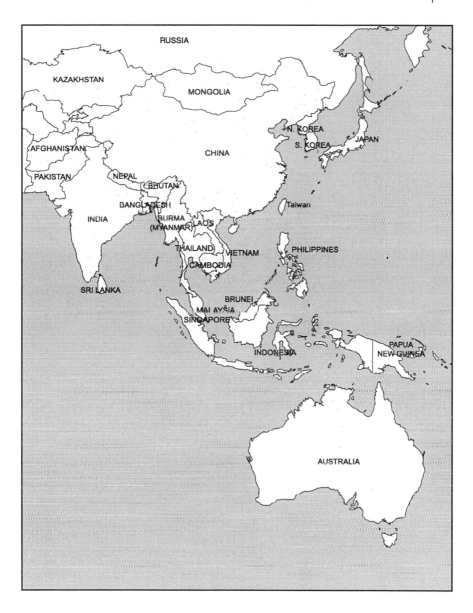

Preface

Graham T. Allison

The Asia-Pacific region has become an increasingly dangerous and uncertain place.[1] As a new century dawns, the strategic situation in Asia remains fraught with old instabilities and new risks. At the same time, fresh opportunities exist to build peace and stability in the region.

This raises the question why America's alliance system in the Asia-Pacific region has not evolved or changed significantly since the end of the Soviet threat. In Asia, the United States and its allies face an arc of potential instability from the divided Korean peninsula in Asia's far northeast, to the nuclear confrontation between India and Pakistan on the South Asian subcontinent, to an unstable Indonesia in Southeast Asia. China's political and ideological conflict with Taiwan threatens to involve the United States in a major interstate military conflict. India is emerging as a major power. Russia retains an influence. The unity of Indonesia, a country of 200 million people, is at risk. The strategic challenges posed by these geopolitical flashpoints are compounded by the proliferation of weapons of mass destruction and the spread of destabilizing high-technology conventional weapons; the problem of expanding the world free trade system; and continuing effects of the 1997–98 Asian financial crisis.

To answer these questions, the Australian American Leadership Dialogue and its founder, Phillip H. Scanlan, asked Robert D. Blackwill of Harvard University's John F. Kennedy School of Government and Paul Dibb of the Australian National University's Research School of

---

1. Because of strategic interconnections among these areas, this book defines the Asia-Pacific region as the continental and maritime countries of Northeast, Southeast, and South Asia, Australasia, and the Pacific islands.

Pacific and Asian Studies to bring together a task force of nine distinguished American and Australian strategists. This book is the result, presenting detailed suggestions for policymakers who must face these old and new challenges.

The central premise of the book is that these challenges can best be met by strengthening America's alliances with Japan, South Korea, and Australia, and by retaining a strong U.S. military presence in the region. The volume offers a series of prescriptions for doing so, aimed at analysts, opinion leaders, and especially policymakers in all four countries.

The editors asked the authors to adopt a five-year time frame, so that their recommendations will address the challenges of the present era without becoming caught in the fast-changing minutiae of day-to-day events.

The book is organized into six chapters. The first chapter, by Australian Paul Dibb, surveys the strategic outlook for the region. It explains how and why the strategic balance in Asia is so risky, and offers a strategic assessment of the next five years. Chapter 2, by American Philip Zelikow, examines the evolution of America's role in Asia. It argues that, for over a century, the United States has presented the countries of Asia with a tempting combination of interest, power, and distance.

The next three chapters focus on each of the alliances individually, each with insights from American and Australian co-authors. Chapter 3, by Australian Stuart Harris and American Richard N. Cooper, addresses the future of the U.S.-Japan alliance in light of the broad set of strategic challenges that now confront Japan. In Chapter 4, American Ralph A. Cossa and Australian Alan Oxley turn to the future of the U.S.-South Korea alliance, looking at both the North Korean threat and recent policy initiatives on the Korean peninsula. Chapter 5, by Australian John Baker and American Douglas H. Paal, examines the future of the U.S.-Australia alliance in the absence of the Cold War threats that have shaped the structure and character of that extremely close relationship to date. The final chapter, by American Robert D. Blackwill, lays out a broad policy action agenda for these three alliances and proposes concrete steps to strengthen and build closer coordination in America's existing alliance system in Asia.

On a number of points the authors disagree with one another. Nonetheless these collaborators are unanimous in seeking to spark an informed policy debate about how best to strengthen these alliances to meet the challenges ahead in the Asia-Pacific region. I especially hope that the new U.S. president and his team, as well as the governments in Canberra, Tokyo, and Seoul, will look carefully at the important analysis and proposed prescriptions in this volume. We at the Kennedy School are delighted to be part of this consequential U.S.-Australia project.

Finally, we wish especially to thank Phillip H. Scanlan, whose original idea stimulated this effort; Evan A. Feigenbaum, the task force Executive Secretary who served as the administrator of the project; and Teresa Lawson, who edited the book.

Graham T. Allison
Director
Belfer Center for Science and International Affairs
John F. Kennedy School of Government
Harvard University

Foreword

Phillip H. Scanlan

At the 1999 World Economic Forum in Davos, a panel discussion addressed the theme that the Asian financial crisis presented "no threat to regional security." The consensus emerged that the U.S. presence in the region had been pivotal in facilitating a prospectively softer economic landing than expected, and remained crucial to safeguarding regional security. However, the informed global audience queried the durability of U.S. commitment to the region. At issue, therefore, was the integrity of the network of U.S. alliances across the Asia-Pacific.

Given this frame of reference, it was natural to request Harvard's John F. Kennedy School of Government, in an academic and intellectual process initiated with the assistance of the Australian American Leadership Dialogue, to conduct a systematic review of U.S. alliances with Japan, Korea, and Australia — each an alliance conceived in circumstances of a bygone era — and of the contemporary strategic signposts in the region. For those of us in Australia who have harbored for a quarter-century the ambition of focusing the best U.S. policy minds on the U.S. alliance with Australia, the time had arrived. The Kennedy School's model of alliance review, already practiced on the Middle East and NATO, seemed an appropriate point of commencement. Joseph Nye, the Dean of Harvard University's Kennedy School of Government, agreed.

The Australian American Leadership Dialogue is a private initiative of citizens from both countries who meet annually to review the parameters of the bilateral relationship. Its uniqueness lies in its bipartisan reach, and the opportunity it presents its participants to transcend domestic political differences and work together to advance the interests of their respective countries. People take part on their own time, not as official representatives of any government or institution.

I am grateful to the collaborative authors from the United States and Australia, especially co-leaders Bob Blackwill and Paul Dibb, for their commitment to the importance and integrity of this Alliance Review. This volume represents the views of the authors alone. It does not reflect the views of the Dialogue itself nor of all those on both sides of the Pacific who have participated in the Australian American Leadership Dialogue; indeed it does not seek to do so. This book is meant to facilitate the best thinking of all who are concerned about these important issues. A premise of the Australian American Leadership Dialogue is that a new generation of leadership inevitably re-examines established ties, and that sustainable relationships demand hard work and constant nurturing. I trust this Alliance Review will provide a sound foundation for many new and constructive dialogues throughout the Asia-Pacific and beyond.

Phillip H. Scanlan
Founder
Australian American Leadership Dialogue

Chapter 1

The Strategic Environment in the Asia-Pacific Region

Paul Dibb

Asia's future security is far from certain. Both optimistic and pessimistic views about the region exist. On the one hand, there is the belief that the future of a peaceful world belongs to Asia and that this region will come to outstrip the United States and Europe in terms of economic power. On the other hand, there is the view that Asia is a particularly dangerous part of the world where there is a risk that major war could occur. The very fact that such different "expert" opinions can be held about Asia should lead us to a great deal of caution about proclaiming with any certainty the region's strategic outlook. In judging the strategic future of Asia, one should learn from previous failures of intelligence assessment and refrain from over-confident, straight-line extrapolations from past experience.

A brief review of just how wrong past strategic pronouncements about Asia have been should demonstrate this point. After North Vietnam's victory over South Vietnam in 1975, there was great fear that communism would spread quickly to the rest of Southeast Asia and that the "dominos" would fall. This did not occur and in fact the countries of the Association of South East Asian Nations (ASEAN) defeated their communist insurgencies and absorbed Vietnam into their membership. In the 1980s, when Japanese economic growth seemed formidable, we were told that the coming "Japanese economic superpower" would soon outstrip the United States in terms of gross national product (GNP). Instead, Japan has recorded barely one-third of the economic growth rate of the United States since 1990. More recently, there have been confident predictions that China will soon be the new economic giant and that its GNP will be bigger than that of the United States by 2010. But by most measures China's economy is only a fraction of that of the United States, and is quickly slowing down as China struggles with the challenge of privatization of the state-owned sector. Until the Asian economic crisis of 1997–98, we were being lectured about the so-called Asian economic miracle and the fact that "Asian values" had found a successful new formula for combining astounding economic growth with political authoritarianism. Instead, we witnessed the collapse of Asian economies such as South Korea's, which had been held up as a paradigm of economic success, and the replacement of the military regime in Indonesia by democracy. At the same time, the West was surprised by the nuclear weapons programs of North Korea, India, and Pakistan.

Asia is one of the most heavily armed regions of the world. There are still many outstanding ideological and territorial disputes in the region. The history of Asia, unlike Europe, is one where hot wars have occurred in the past half-century. The Second World War was followed quickly by the outbreak of war in Korea and the succession of wars with Vietnam. There was also war between India and Pakistan in the early 1970s, as well as anti-communist guerrilla campaigns in most Southeast Asian countries, and military confrontation by Indonesia in the early 1960s. While the recent history of Asia has been more peaceful, it has not prevented the use of armed force in Cambodia, Kashmir, Sri Lanka, East Timor, Bougainville, and the South China Sea; nor in territorial disputes between North and South Korea, the Koreas and Japan, China and Japan, and China and Taiwan. The strategic situation in Asia is tenser and less peaceful than anywhere in Europe, apart from the former Yugoslavia.

The euphoria in Washington after the collapse of the Soviet Union and the end of the Warsaw Pact led the United States to premature optimism about the emergence of a peaceful and cooperative new world order. This benign view of the world was reinforced by the remarkable economic growth of Asia and the development of multilateral institutions such as the Asia Pacific Economic Cooperation (APEC) forum and the ASEAN Regional Forum (ARF). But these institutions have shown themselves to be weak when confronted with major regional problems such as the Asian economic crisis and the independence of East Timor. Moreover, the emergence of major powers such as China and India, Japan's failure to exert a regional leadership role, and Russia's potential to align itself with China all present the United States with a much more dynamic and potentially unstable strategic situation in Asia than in Europe.

The Geopolitics of Asia

There is a fashionable view in some of the contemporary international relations literature that geography and geopolitics are no longer relevant in the post–Cold War strategic era. This is demonstrably untrue in Asia, where great distances, enormous variations in culture and civilization, and the struggle for power and influence among the region's great powers fundamentally define Asia's strategic outlook. While it is the case that globalization and the information technology revolution are having an increasing impact on the trade and commerce of Asia, and even — some would argue — on the democratization of the politics of the region, Asia retains many of the geopolitical elements of the Cold War. Moreover, the geography of Asia still has a considerable influence on the military forces and strategic preoccupations of regional powers.

In the north of the region, there are three great continental land powers: China, India, and Russia. China and India each have more than one billion people and their armed forces are very large: 2.5 million in the case of China and 1.2 million for India. Both China and India are ambitious powers. They are already the predominant military powers in Northeast Asia and South Asia, respectively, and they both have nuclear weapons. In the future, China and India will expand their military reach beyond their immediate neighborhoods. They are natural competitors for power and influence in the leadership of the region. As their economies continue to grow strongly, they will be able to afford more modern defense forces, including significant elements of naval power. Their strategic ambitions will overlap in Southeast Asia; this is an area of great strategic significance for U.S. allies — especially Japan — because half the world's sea-borne trade passes through it. Russia is now a greatly weakened power, but it retains a global nuclear reach and the technological capacity to provide advanced conventional weapons to both China and India; it thus has a considerable influence on the future balance of power in the region. Russia's geography enables it to have, as the United States does not, a physical presence in Northeast Asia, where its Siberian and Far Eastern provinces share a common border with China. In the longer term, beyond the next five years, it would be foolish to discount the potential for rise of Russia's military capabilities and a strongly anti-Western strategic posture.

These three great continental powers are flanked by an arc of maritime and archipelagic powers, all of which are much smaller in terms of population and military power. It is in this maritime strategic environment that America's allies and close friends are located: Japan, South Korea, Taiwan, Thailand, Singapore, the Philippines, Australia, and New Zealand. Some of America's most important allies are in close proximity to the military power of China and Russia. This group includes Japan, which is greatly dependent upon maritime trade for its economic survival; South Korea, which is highly vulnerable to a short-warning North Korean military attack; and Taiwan, which is increasingly overshadowed by the growth of China's military power and its political ambitions to absorb the island into the mainland. Another group of America's allies and close friends lies at a greater distance from the three large continental powers and, therefore, should be less susceptible to great-power pressure. But this group includes some small and middle-size powers — for instance, Thailand and the Philippines — that will find it hard to resist the pressure of the rise of China to power. There is a general perception in the region that Southeast Asia, flanked by Australia, is not as important strategically to the United States as is Northeast Asia.

In the past, South Asia has been much less important to the strategic interests of the United States (and its allies in the Asia-Pacific region) than either Northeast Asia or Southeast Asia. Pakistan, which was a useful counterweight to the Soviet military presence in Afghanistan, is now much more of a strategic liability to Western interests given its connections to Muslim extremists, its development of nuclear weapons, and its military alignment with China. The world's largest democracy, India, could become of much greater strategic significance to the United States as a counterweight to the rise of Chinese military power, but for this to occur, India will have to expand out of its narrow strategic vision, which remains obsessively focused on Pakistan. America and its allies, including Australia, will need to monitor closely the development of India's naval power and its ambitions in the Indian Ocean in the longer term.

The political make-up of Asia is highly varied, and this adds to the geopolitical complexity of the region. Unlike Europe, where a broad swath of democratic countries occupies most of the continent, Asia still has four of the world's five remaining communist countries: China, North Korea, Vietnam, and Laos. And while there has been an encouraging rise of democracy in recent years in South Korea, Taiwan, Thailand, the Philippines, and now in Indonesia, authoritarian regimes are in power in China, North Korea, Vietnam, Burma, and Pakistan. It remains to be seen whether the military, which has effectively ruled Indonesia for the last thirty-five years, will easily relinquish power to a truly democratic government. In any case, the trend to democracy in Asia — if it continues — does not necessarily imply easier relationships with the United States, as the New Zealand case demonstrates. The global trend in the post–Cold War era is toward a narrower definition of national interest and a greater focus on immediate regional concerns. The U.S. alliance system in the Asia-Pacific region will need to counter this trend if the sharing of values that has been built up over the last fifty years is to continue.

Asia is characterized by strongly nationalist governments. Absent a sudden collapse of the regime in Pyongyang, communism is not about to disappear in North Korea. While there may well be a gradual softening of communist political control in both China and Vietnam, hard-line nationalism has recently replaced communism in the political posture of China. The persistence of democracy in India has not made dealing with that country any easier for the Western alliance. The highly questionable proposition that democracies do not go to war with democracies, which has become an article of faith in some quarters in the United States, may be disproved in Asia. Deep-seated historical, cultural, religious, and territorial differences in Asia suggest that — irrespective of the development of democratic institutions — the risks of armed conflict remain. The shallowness of multilateral organizations such as APEC and the ASEAN Regional Forum, and their inability to resolve regional crises, only adds to the sense of caution.

In short, fundamental change — certainly over the next five years and most probably even over the next decade — is not likely in the geopolitical makeup of Asia. Many of the divides of the Cold War period will remain intact, short of catastrophic change in North Korea or

China. Even where favorable change does occur, it could bring with it a strong sense of nationalism: for example, in a unified Korea.

As the Revolution in Military Affairs (RMA) spreads to Asia and introduces longer-range and more accurate weapons, supported by real-time intelligence and surveillance information, this may compress the geography of Asia. The introduction of long-range cruise missiles and the development of ballistic missiles equipped with nuclear warheads will make the geography of the region less relevant, and it will also make smaller countries much more vulnerable if deterrence fails. The risk then will be either a retaliatory proliferation of ballistic missiles, or the acquisition from the United States of a protective ballistic missile defense, which in turn may lead to the multiplication of offensive missile systems. There are now more nuclear weapons powers in the Asia-Pacific region than in any other part of the world: they are held, or thought to be held, by Russia, China, India, Pakistan, and North Korea, as well as the United States. The nuclear weapons proliferation challenge for the United States and its allies will be more acute in Asia than anywhere else.

Although these developments will bring about fundamental changes to the military geography of Asia, the location and historical experience of many of the region's countries will mean that their strategic postures and perceptions of threat will not change. Thus, while China and India may well develop greater strategic reach — and in the longer term more capable blue-water navies — their fundamental strategic concerns with their neighbors, as well as with each other, will not diminish the importance they attach to large standing armies. China now sees Japan as more of a threat than Russia, but this will not cause it to leave its northern borders defenseless. Nevertheless, a weak Russia has enabled China for the first time in centuries to focus more on its eastern approaches and its strategic ambitions in the South China Sea. Japan, as a result, now sees China as much more of a long-term threat than Russia. Whether Japan and China can come to some sort of strategic accommodation, or whether instead their rivalry will lead to conflict, will fundamentally determine the geopolitical balance in Asia. Although an accommodation between Japan and China would clearly be preferable, it would not be to the benefit of the Western alliance system if it involved a strategic partnership between Asia's two greatest powers. Similarly, if a "triple entente" were to emerge between China,

Russia, and India, it would threaten the entire stability of the region. Neither of these scenarios is at all likely.

In the next five years, the military forces of most countries in the region will remain fundamentally unchanged. Given the long lead-times for the acquisition of major items of military equipment, such as surface warships and advanced fighter aircraft, their military power five years from now will not be much different from their current orders of battle. The exception will be the continuing enhancement of U.S. capabilities.

Over a ten-year period, however, change will be more substantial. In particular, there will be smaller, more mobile armies, with less emphasis on high-intensity armored warfare. There will also be a greater trend toward amphibious troops for the protection of offshore territories and assets. Acquiring modern navies and air forces is becoming increasingly expensive as the cost of each new generation of military equipment approximately doubles (both to acquire and to operate). This will make it difficult for small and middle-sized powers — including all of the countries of Southeast Asia with the exception of Singapore — to retain a basic defensive capability. Larger countries, especially Japan, will be able to afford and will have access to U.S. technology that will enable them to remain at the forefront of military capabilities. China, however, is likely to struggle: it will be able to acquire small numbers of sophisticated conventional weapons from Russia, but it will have trouble maintaining them. Over the next decade, neither China nor India will have a real-time, long-range offensive strike capability that in any way resembles the current U.S. capability, or even that of ten years ago.

The real question for U.S. allies is not whether the United States will continue to be the dominant world military power, but whether they as allies will be able to keep up with U.S. military forces in terms of interoperability of communications and weapons systems. The United States will be reluctant to share some of its sensitive RMA secrets even with its closest friends. But if it does not, then its key allies in the Asia-Pacific — Japan, South Korea, and Australia in particular — cannot be expected to carry more of the allied burden in the region because they will not have compatible militaries capable of coordinating with U.S. military technologies.

Strategic developments in Asia are not likely to pose fundamental challenges to U.S. military power and influence, as long as the United States retains a credible forward military presence and is not found wanting if there is a major military crisis involving its allies. For its allies, however, the situation is likely to be much more demanding because the region has become more fluid and complex and much less predictable. America's allies need to develop — as a first priority — military forces that are credible in their own immediate neighborhoods and which can also offer a useful contribution to U.S. operations further afield.

The geographical diversity of regional crises in the post–Cold War era means that the United States is going to be much more stretched in terms of its military capabilities. There are now reasonable doubts about whether the United States can cope militarily with two major regional crises almost simultaneously — for example, on the Korean peninsula at the same time as a major regional war in the Middle East.

The Short-term Strategic Outlook

Despite the Asian economic crisis of 1997–98, defense spending in the Asia-Pacific region remains robust. Total defense expenditure in the region amounts to about $150 billion a year and grew by 25 percent in real terms between 1985 and 1998. The Asia-Pacific region spends more on defense than any other part of the world except the United States and NATO Europe (which spend about $265 billion per year and $170 billion per year, respectively, on defense). By far the largest share of regional defense spending occurs in Northeast Asia, which accounts for almost 70 percent of the total. This is where the largest military powers are and where there are significant military tensions. China and Japan are among the top four or five military spenders in the world, each having a defense budget of almost $40 billion a year.

TAIWAN STRAIT

The most dangerous part of Northeast Asia at present is the Taiwan Strait. There seems to be an inevitable progression in the domestic politics of Taiwan that seeks to assert Taiwan's international status as an independent state and to confront China's "one-China policy." The situation is exacerbated by growing tensions between the United States and China over this issue, as well as distrust in Washington over

China's nuclear weapons program and in Beijing over the U.S. desire to deploy a national and theater ballistic missile defense capability. Tension over these issues brings with it a real risk of miscalculation. China lacks the conventional military capabilities to mount an amphibious invasion of Taiwan and this will remain the case for at least the next five years. But there are other options open to China, including a naval blockade and the use of ballistic missiles. War across the Taiwan Strait would, inevitably, bring in the United States, and would involve enormously difficult choices for U.S. allies, particularly Japan, but also Australia. Although China would eventually have to come to terms with the United States after such a conflict, it would not have to do so with others. China's relations with Japan — in the event of Japanese military support for the United States — would become permanently hostile, while it would treat Australia, a distant small power, with contempt and long-term isolation. Hence there is a strong desire by U.S. allies in the Asia-Pacific region to see the current tensions between China and the United States over Taiwan resolved by peaceful means.

THE KOREAN PENINSULA
The situation on the Korean peninsula remains tense, as it has been for almost fifty years. The risk of a North Korean attack on the South is ever-present, but the outbreak of war is unlikely. Unlike the early 1950s, North Korea could not now count on military support from China and Russia. It would face the bleak prospect of total defeat by the United States, perhaps by the use of nuclear weapons. Miscalculation by the paranoid North Korean regime cannot be discounted, nor can a sudden collapse of the North, which would present South Korea with the horrendous costs of creating a unified Korea. One estimate puts the cost of reunification as equal to one-third of South Korea's annual budget over a decade or more. The most likely scenario over the next five years is a continuation of manageable tension, with no real progress towards a negotiated, peaceful settlement. Should war break out, however, the United States would expect its allies quickly to provide useful military contributions. If in these circumstances Japan were to refuse to give tangible military assistance, such a refusal would undoubtedly put at risk the continuation of the U.S.-Japan alliance.

OTHER FLASHPOINTS IN NORTHEAST ASIA

There are other potential flashpoints in Northeast Asia: the offshore territorial disputes between North and South Korea, Japan and South Korea, and Japan and China. They may generate limited military confrontations, but are unlikely to result in dangerous military situations. Such territorial disputes could be used as an excuse for the expression of nationalism, especially by China. Of greater concern is the development of the balance of power, which is perceived in the region as having moved in favor of China. But China's real power will remain more political, and to an extent economic, than military. Japan is likely to remain preoccupied with its serious domestic economic problems and to have only a limited ability to provide a regional counterweight to the emergence of Chinese power. Over the next five years, Russia's power in Northeast Asia will remain weak, and North and South Korea will continue to be preoccupied with each other. This situation underlines the importance of the U.S.-Japan alliance and the U.S. forward military position in Northeast Asia.

SOUTH ASIA

The second-largest concentration of military power in the region is in South Asia, where India and Pakistan have been in confrontation with each other since their creation as separate states in 1947. The possession of nuclear weapons by both these countries and their development of long-range ballistic missiles presents a situation of great danger. Their religious and territorial differences and the fact that the military balance between them is moving in favor of India will result in a highly dangerous scenario in which the use of nuclear weapons is a real risk. There is a grave lack of early-warning technologies and nuclear weapon command and control arrangements in both countries.

It is time that India was taken more seriously by the international community. India could come to play a much more significant role in the emerging balance of power in Asia. But to do this India would have to lift its strategic horizons out of the narrow confines of the subcontinent and recognize that its continuing obsession with nonalignment is quaint and irrelevant. Russia is now a weak ally of India, while China is a hostile competitor. If India is to become a real player in Asia, it should accept these facts of life and improve its relations with that other great democracy, the United States.

SOUTHEAST ASIA

Southeast Asia has a population of over 500 million and it contains the world's fourth largest country, Indonesia. But Southeast Asia is not as important strategically to the United States as either Northeast Asia or South Asia. This region contains no great powers, although Indonesia and Vietnam have long-term potential as very important middle powers. Since the end of the Vietnam War in 1975, the risk of major interstate conflict in Southeast Asia has disappeared. Moreover, until the economic crisis of 1997–98, Southeast Asia was a model of economic growth, and its regional body — ASEAN — served as an important stabilizing influence, putting minor regional conflicts to one side and concentrating on political harmony. However, the Asian economic crisis and the political upheaval in Indonesia have greatly weakened Southeast Asia and shown how ineffectual ASEAN is. Over the next five years, ASEAN is likely to be preoccupied with holding together its disparate membership of ten countries, which range from an oppressive military regime in Burma to emerging democracies in the Philippines and Thailand.

The central question for Southeast Asia is whether the world's fourth largest country, Indonesia, will remain a cohesive nation-state or whether it will disintegrate along the lines of the former Yugoslavia. There is a better than even chance that Indonesia will muddle through and retain its basic territorial integrity, although Aceh, Maluku, and West Irian (West Papua) are high-risk situations. Were Indonesia to disintegrate, the implications for neighboring countries — and especially for Singapore, Malaysia, the Philippines, Papua New Guinea, and Australia — would be serious. Relations between Indonesia and Australia — which is America's closest ally in the entire Asia-Pacific region — have become very strained.

The stability of Southeast Asia should have more salience in Washington than it seems now to have. Over half of the world's maritime trade passes through the confined waters of Southeast Asia. As the naval power of China grows, there will be increased anxiety in the region about the security of vital sea lines of communication through Southeast Asian waters. The most dangerous part of Southeast Asia is the South China Sea, where there are overlapping territorial claims by China (which claims all the islands and reefs), Taiwan, Vietnam, Malaysia, Brunei, the Philippines, and Indonesia. The United States is not a party principal to these territorial disputes, but it must make it clear to China that it will not tolerate Chinese territorial hegemony over the South China Sea. Regular demonstrations of the superior naval capabilities of the United States and its allies will be important reminders to China that its proper course of action is a negotiated one with the countries of Southeast Asia.

AUSTRALIA, NEW ZEALAND, AND THE SOUTH PACIFIC ISLANDS

Australia, New Zealand, and the South Pacific islands are the most stable part of the Asia-Pacific region. Australia is the predominant power in this part of the world and, until recently, there was confidence that the strategic circumstances of Australia's immediate neighborhood were benign. While there is no prospect of a major challenge to Australia's security over the next five years, an arc of instability now extends to the north and east of Australia. Indonesia's highly uncertain future presents a potential major strategic challenge to Australia: Australia's national interests favor a unified Indonesia, but the future cohesion of the vast Indonesian archipelago is now very uncertain. Papua New Guinea, which shares a common border with Indonesia, is a weak state with a fragile economy, high levels of corruption and violence, and an active secessionist movement in Bougainville. The peoples of Papua New Guinea and West Irian share a common Melanesian ethnic origin and a distrust of Indonesia. In the event of conflict between Indonesia and its West Irian province over independence, Papua New Guinea — which has a security treaty with Australia — would side with its Melanesian brothers. The risk of conflict between Australia and Indonesia would then rise. If, however, Indonesia were to grant greater autonomy to West Irian, this contingency should be averted. Several of the South Pacific islands close to Australia and New Zealand are scarcely viable economically and have regimes noted for their corruption, in particular the Solomon Islands and Vanuatu. New Zealand is Australia's oldest ally and these two countries have fought alongside each other in most of the military conflicts of the last century, from the Boer War to Vietnam. But since the mid-1980s, New Zealand has drifted out of the ANZUS alliance and it has cut its defense capabilities so that it is capable of little other than peacekeeping operations. Canberra will increasingly come to see New Zealand as more of a liability than a useful ally.

THE OVERALL STRATEGIC SITUATION IN THE ASIA-PACIFIC REGION

The Asia-Pacific region has entered a particularly complex and fluid strategic situation. The Asian economic crisis, tension between China and the United States over Taiwan, North Korea's nuclear and ballistic missile programs, the risk of war between India and Pakistan, and the potential for Indonesia to disintegrate have all occurred suddenly, and serve to underline the basic insecurity of the region. With the crucial exception of Taiwan, none of these situations presents the danger of major power war. Over the next five years, U.S. allies in the Asia-Pacific region are unlikely to be faced with serious direct military threat. War across the Taiwan Strait, however, would present them with most unpalatable choices about supporting the United States militarily. It is unlikely that the forward U.S. military presence in the region will change significantly over the next five years. Modest adjustments to the current forward basing of about 100,000 troops may well occur as technology enables the United States to replace "boots on the ground" with stand-off weapons. But short of unification of the Korean peninsula, such adjustments will not herald any substantial U.S. withdrawal. However, there is uncertainty about the future direction of U.S. policies; this is a central theme of later chapters of this book and one to which we now turn.

Uncertain U.S. Policies

U.S. political power and military presence is the key to maintaining a peaceful balance of power in Asia over the next five years. Only America has the power, credibility, and distance from the region to maintain the regional balance of power. Other contenders for this role would not be acceptable to the regional powers. China is feared as a potential dominant — and perhaps expansionist — power. Great suspicion still surrounds any ambitions for regional leadership that Japan might have. India is seen as essentially peripheral to East Asian affairs. Russia is a weak and distracted power.

U.S. credibility is based not only on its regional military presence, but also on its long historical ties to the region over the last hundred years. Most countries in the region, apart from China, fear that an Asia without the United States would be a much more dangerous place. It would leave the regional balance of power open to fierce contention between China and Japan and between China and India, possibly leading to war. But the United States is much more distracted these days by domestic events and by its focus on Europe. It is also much more stretched; it must react to the outbreak of regional crises across the globe with a military force that is little more than half the size it was in the Cold War. There are now serious doubts in the region whether the United States can fulfill its much-vaunted East Asian strategy: that is, to handle two regional conflicts "almost simultaneously." A failure by the United States to handle a major crisis in, for example, the Korean peninsula at the same time as it was fighting a regional crisis elsewhere, for example in the Middle East, would be disastrous for the alliance system. The United States is the only nation with the power to enforce security across the region. No reasonable ally, however, can expect the United States to be a perfect arbiter and enforcer of security, and indeed, there is a growing perception that the United States tends to carry out its military duties only after armed conflict has broken out. The Gulf War is the obvious example, along with Bosnia-Herzegovina and Serbia-Kosovo.

This uncertainty over the speed of U.S. response has consequences for those countries in Asia that expect the United States to maintain regional peace and security. Many in Asia believe that the United States will not necessarily be there, except for Korea, at the moment when conflict breaks out. It may — depending on the degree of strategic interest and the nature of domestic reaction — turn up quickly, and it might ultimately restore the status quo, but this will be little comfort for nations whose territory has been attacked in the meantime. Moreover, the manner in which the United States intervenes will be strongly shaped by domestic considerations: it will seek to respond to an armed conflict in the most domestically acceptable way, in other words, with air power. But in the more likely Northeast Asian scenarios, such as those concerning Korea and perhaps Taiwan, a ground force will be essential to restore the status quo.

Strategic inconsistency has also been evident in the U.S. response to the Asian economic crisis. Asia's multilateral institutions — the APEC forum, ASEAN, and the ASEAN Regional Forum (ARF) — failed to play any role in addressing the crisis, underscoring the extent to which regional economic and strategic stability depends heavily on the policies and initiatives of the United States. This means that Asia's welfare depends critically on the depth of strategic understanding in Washing-

ton. But it appears that U.S. policymakers still weigh strategic significance in Cold War terms: South Korea received quick and significant
economic assistance because it faced a communist North armed with
nuclear weapons, but Indonesia did not, because, with the Cold War
over, the world's fourth largest country is no longer important to the
United States as a bastion against communism.

The United States does not appear to have developed a replacement
standard by which to measure the strategic significance of countries
such as Indonesia. Washington let the International Monetary Fund
(IMF) impose dangerously destabilizing measures on Jakarta, including removal of the national subsidy on fuel and the government's mo-
nopoly on the distribution of basic food commodities. Human rights
rather than geopolitics appear to dominate the U.S.-Indonesia relationship today. While human rights issues have an undeniably important
place in international diplomacy, they are of little concern at present to
a vast nation such as Indonesia struggling to maintain its social and
political cohesion. For the sake of the stability of the whole of Southeast Asia, the United States needs to focus on the critical importance of
Indonesian unity and cohesion.

A decade after the Cold War ended, it is time for Washington to develop a more refined process for assessing the strategic significance of
events in Asia, and hence for deciding the weight to be given in its
policy and economic responses to pivotal episodes that will determine
the region's future. Where the United States can do much better is in its
policy response to events such as the Asian economic crisis and the
recent upheaval in Indonesia. It should cease allocating its economic
and political support on the basis of Cold War strategic values, and
devise new tenets for its strategic engagement policy in Asia.

Strategic Shocks and Discontinuities

Given the uncertainties outlined above, U.S. security planners and
their allied opposite numbers need to prepare for alternative, less benign strategic futures in Asia, rather than relying on comfortable predictions that the region will promptly return to economic growth and
therefore to political stability and peace. It may, and there are some
encouraging signs of a return to economic growth in South Korea,
Thailand, and Malaysia — but not in Indonesia. Asia is still vulnerable

to a second economic shock, given that most countries in the region have not corrected their problems with corruption and lack of transparency in their financial markets. This would have a profoundly destabilizing impact on the entire region, particularly if it involved Japan or China. Strong economic growth, on the other hand, would serve to accelerate the acquisition of arms in the region and so present new security challenges. There was a 25 percent real increase in defense expenditure in the Asia-Pacific over the period 1985–98. If this trend continues, the region will be spending almost $200 billion a year on defense by 2010. This will greatly complicate the defense planning of America's allies and make it much more difficult for them to maintain the traditional margin of technological superiority that they have enjoyed for many decades. Allied defense budgets will at least have to keep pace with the regional trend, and allies will need to work much harder at technological cooperation if they are to maintain a degree of interoperability with the United States that is in any way usable.

Our strategic analysis does not predict the likelihood of major power war in the Asia-Pacific region over the next five years, unless the Taiwan situation erupts. But we do see a region in the throes of a painful transformation to renewed economic growth and — in the longer term — to a new balance of power. China's rise to power is, in particular, a great unknown: will it be a peaceful and cooperative power, or will it be belligerent and expansionist? It would be unwise in these circumstances for policymakers to have any confidence in predicting a single view of the strategic future. The strategic shocks of the future may be totally unlike those of the past. Neither is it certain that regimes thought to be stable, such as the former Indonesia or the current regimes in Burma or North Korea, will not be suddenly overthrown. It is safer to predict that there are unlikely to be more nuclear powers in Asia in five years than there are now.

The most important message emerging from our analysis, however, is that U.S. allies need to do more together, given the fluidity of the strategic situation in Asia and the speed with which events unfold there. There is no doubt about the fundamental economic strength of the United States and its allies in the region and the military superiority of the U.S. alliance system. Of much greater concern is the cohesion of the U.S. alliances in the post–Cold War era and the political will of Western leaders to use force if confronted with real military adventurism in the Asia-Pacific region. The areas of maximum danger and instability in the world today are in Northeast Asia and South Asia, followed by the Middle East and parts of the former Soviet Union. Any perception of a wavering or ambiguous U.S. military commitment to the Asia-Pacific region could lead to rapidly heightened risks of destabilization.

There is no unifying enemy to keep the United States and its allies together in the same way as when the threat from the Soviet Union existed. Yet the NATO alliance has adjusted to the lack of a clear enemy by rejuvenating its charter and expanding its membership. Will U.S. allies in the Asia-Pacific region also come up with a new common security concept? Or will the lack of a common threat lead to a gradual weakening of the well-tried ties that bind the United States in its bilateral alliances with Australia, Japan, and South Korea? Rather than threat based, the alliance emphasis in the Asia-Pacific must now be on shared interests in the maintenance of regional stability. This book addresses these issues because they are vital to the question of whether the U.S. alliance system in Asia will continue to endure in the years ahead.

Chapter 2

American Engagement in Asia

Philip Zelikow

The standard narrative of U.S. foreign policy in the twentieth century has the following oft-repeated myths.

- The United States started the century as a growing economic giant that shunned overseas political and military engagement, except to police its own hemisphere.

- The United States was pulled, with some reluctance, into World War I and then forsook its global responsibilities and returned to isolation in the 1920s and 1930s, leaving a void that fired the dangerous ambitions of the dictators.

- Having refused to organize opposition to the dictators in the late 1930s, the United States was drawn reluctantly into World War II.

- After World War II the United States learned its lesson and, in the late 1940s, finally agreed that its economic and military might must be committed to the containment of communism. Substantial and enduring multilateral institutions were built to cement this commitment.

- The Cold War ended with the triumph of democratic ideals and the decline of forcible coercion. Despite the resurfacing of some nasty, lingering ethnic conflicts, the patterns of cooperation and multilateral institutions built during the Cold War have created a reasonably stable equilibrium so that there is little danger of war involving the great powers.

Readers will notice that this narrative is mainly a simplification of the story of U.S. policy toward Europe. But most U.S. policymakers and intellectuals (and of course their students) know little about the history of U.S. foreign policy in any other part of the world. So they tend to equate the story of America and Europe with the story of America and the world. This is a fundamental mistake.

The Real Story

To understand U.S. engagement in Asia, first we must discard the standard narrative. On that side of the world, each element of the story has played out differently.

MYTH NO. 1

The first myth is that "the United States started the century as a growing economic giant that shunned overseas political and military engagement, except to police its own hemisphere." Yet in Asia, the United States began the century as an imperial power. Years earlier the United States had gained control over Hawaii under circumstances that can, charitably, be described as undemocratic. Having extended its domain to the Philippines by the military conquest of that remnant of the Spanish Empire, the United States proceeded to win a bitter colonial war to subjugate the native Filipinos. Meanwhile, on the Asian mainland, U.S. troops were joining those of other empires in killing Chinese rebels — the Boxers — and marching to Beijing. In 1905, the U.S. president served as the mediator in helping end the war between Russia and Japan for control of Manchuria. The United States was urging an "open door" for all in China. In other words, the America of 1900 was a country widely and deeply engaged in the affairs of Asia.

MYTH NO. 2

The second myth is that "the United States was pulled, with some reluctance, into World War I and then forsook its global responsibilities and returned to isolation in the 1920s and 1930s, leaving a void that fired the dangerous ambitions of the dictators." Yet in Asia, there was no World War I, except for some scavenging of German possessions. Japan was the ally of Great Britain, which in turn became America's ally in 1917.

More important, while the United States was renouncing the League of Nations in Europe, it was doing just the opposite in Asia. There, the United States was creating the new international order. Historians call the resulting structure the "Washington conference system," or just the "Washington system." This was a comprehensive attempt to create a multinational system of cooperation in Asia, underpinned by political, military, and economic agreements. Every major power agreed to take part (except for Soviet Russia). In this system, which was fully in place by 1922, a balance of military power was secured by naval treaties between the United States, Britain, and Japan (Washington 1922, London 1930). Economic stability was secured by common adherence to the gold standard. Political cooperation was founded on the Nine Power Treaty, in which eight powers promised the ninth, China, that they would uphold its independence and integrity, maintain equal economic opportunity, and provide an environment for development of a stable Chinese government. The United States reinforced these ideals by its own moves toward decolonization, agreeing in 1934 to move ahead with independence for the Philippines.

Japan's ambitions in Asia did not arise from the withdrawal of the United States from international engagement. Quite the contrary, "the revolt against the Washington Conference system may, paradoxically, be viewed as evidence that the system had steadily become strengthened; those opposed to it would have to resort to drastic measures to undermine it."[1] Japan began to define its new political identity as a reaction against the *dominance* of the Washington system and the internationalist, Western ideals Japan thought it symbolized. In the superheated and sometimes violent arguments within Tokyo in the 1920s and early 1930s, army and navy officers, right-wing politicians (including some members of the nobility and the imperial family), and reactionary intellectuals felt desperate. They saw venerated tradition undermined by modernity. They saw democracy undermining imperial authority, and they shivered with nightmares of angry peasants on the farms and Bolshevized workers in the newly industrialized cities. They saw Japan's economy and even its sovereignty falling under the control of outsiders, and thought time was running out.

MYTH NO. 3
The third myth is that, "having refused to organize opposition to the dictators in the late 1930s, the United States was drawn reluctantly into World War II." Yet in Asia, the United States had always been in the

---

1. Akira Iriye, *The Origins of the Second World War in Asia and the Pacific* (New York: Longman, 1987), pp. 4–5.

frontline. When Japan's divided and unstable governments began tearing down the Washington system (1931–36), the United States was at least as active as any other power in trying to find peaceful counters. Washington had refused to recognize the Japanese occupation of Manchuria. Although the United States had let its army dwindle in the 1930s and was therefore disparaged by Germany, it had maintained its military posture in Asia, building ships right up to its treaty limits and rejecting Japan's demands for parity. The pathbreaking first U.S. initiative to begin joint military planning with the British (in late 1937) was aimed at Japan, not Germany, a response to Japan's widened war against China and the first killings of U.S. servicemen, on the hapless gunboat *Panay*. It was the British who were reluctant. That same pattern of U.S. military and diplomatic leadership in organizing and supporting resistance to aggression held right through 1941 — in Asia.

Most striking of all, even though the calamities of 1940 led President Franklin D. Roosevelt to agree with Winston Churchill that Germany was the more important enemy, some of his civilian advisers — fixated on their outrage about Japanese moves — could not restrain themselves. In the late summer of 1941 they fashioned an oil embargo out of the minutiae of export licensing decisions, confronting Roosevelt with a fait accompli that he could not disavow.[2] Such moves, along with complacent assumptions about the Japanese, made war in Asia and the Pacific much more likely at the very time when the last thing America's top political and military leaders wanted, in their grand strategy, was for war to start in Asia before it started against Germany.

---

2. Fearing premature war in the Pacific, President Roosevelt repeatedly ruled out an oil embargo, even after Japan moved to occupy southern Indochina in July 1941. Treasury Secretary Henry Morgenthau and Interior Secretary Harold Ickes took advantage of Roosevelt's absence (at the Argentia summit meeting with Churchill) to enlist the help of Assistant Secretary of State Dean Acheson in order to outmaneuver the president and the top officials at the State Department. For a restrained account, see Michael A. Barnhart, *Japan Prepares for Total War* (Ithaca: Cornell University Press, 1987), pp. 224–232 (including notes 42, 46, and 48). Aside from their ire about Japan's violations of international law, these officials also wanted to deter the Japanese from joining with the Germans and declaring war against the Soviet Union (an option that was indeed being seriously advocated by some in Tokyo). In this respect they succeeded all too well, since the option of attacking the Soviet Union was shelved in favor of concentrating on the "southern" option instead.

Nevertheless, that is just what the United States got at Pearl Harbor. Fortunately, Roosevelt was bailed out four days later by Hitler's declaration of war against the United States: it could then be Germany first, after all.

MYTH NO. 4

The fourth myth is that, "after World War II, the United States learned its lesson and, in the late 1940s, finally agreed that its economic and military might must be committed to the containment of communism. Substantial and enduring multilateral institutions were built to cement this commitment." In Europe, the United States was deciding to engage with the Marshall Plan (and its institutions, which evolved into the Organization for Economic Cooperation and Development [OECD]) and then with the North Atlantic Treaty (and its institutions, which evolved into NATO). At the same time, Washington was making the biggest *non*intervention decision of the entire Cold War — in Asia. There, the United States decided it would not attempt to keep communism from taking over China. This decision surprised many Americans who remembered that their country had gone to war with Japan precisely because Washington refused to stand by and accept the loss of China. (And such a loss was not calculated in dollars: after all, in 1940 the United States had much larger stakes of trade and investment in Japan than it did in China.) The United States had invested blood and treasure in China's future for decades. Mao Zedong himself had expected the United States to commit a million troops to save China from communism, and confided this fear to Stalin. Instead, between 1947 and 1949, the United States decided to accept the communist victory in China. In Washington, the priority was now decidedly Europe first.

Stop now, for a moment, and reflect on why Europe and Asia had been treated so differently in U.S. foreign policy for generations. The United States had always been entangled with Europe, but many Americans defined themselves with a conscious separateness from the "Old World" and its troubles. Many of these same Americans saw Asia as a region of hope and opportunity, economic, political, and spiritual — of merchants and missionaries. This was not all.

Before the current era of imagined omnipotence, and especially before the 1960s, U.S. policymakers lived with a sense of scarcity, especially in military power. So they generally felt that they had to choose to commit their scarce military resources either to one side of the world or to the other: there was just not enough to allow the United States to act energetically on both sides of the world. These choices are often mislabeled (by opponents) as isolationism. But an isolationist toward Europe might actually be an internationalist toward Asia. Indeed, the most influential isolationist in U.S. politics in the early postwar years was Robert Taft, the leading Republican in the U.S. Senate. Though Taft is known for his efforts to keep U.S. soldiers out of Europe, he was ready to support vast American commitments in Asia, backing Douglas MacArthur, for instance. (MacArthur himself practically detested Europe, and its governments.) When the political winds later shifted leftward, the leading spokesman for pulling troops out of Europe in the 1970s was the Democratic Senate majority leader, Mike Mansfield. Yet Mansfield ardently supported active American engagement in Asia.

The "Europe first" emphasis of the early Cold War, and the corresponding reluctance to confront communist moves in Asia, ultimately produced considered U.S. decisions in 1949 *not* to defend Taiwan, South Korea, or Indochina with U.S. forces. U.S. forces were withdrawn from South Korea. The new defense perimeter was announced by the secretary of state in early 1950. Unfortunately, these judgments apparently accelerated Soviet, Chinese, and North Korean planning to press the offensive against all three places. Korea came first. Then, to the surprise of almost everyone (including Douglas MacArthur), all these U.S. judgments were promptly reversed. The shock and embarrassment of the North Korean invasion, and the fears for what might then happen in Europe, simply jolted the United States right back into the Asian commitments it had foresworn. But, despite later efforts, the United States never built up political, economic, or military institutions in Asia of a strength and durability comparable to those created in Europe.

MYTH NO. 5

The fifth myth is that "the Cold War ended with the triumph of democratic ideals and the decline of forcible coercion. Despite the resurfacing of some nasty, lingering ethnic conflicts, the patterns of cooperation and multilateral institutions built during the Cold War have created a reasonably stable equilibrium, so that there is little danger of war involving the great powers."

In Europe, the Cold War ended in 1990 with the end of Soviet coercion in Eastern Europe, a treaty creating a united Germany in the Western alliance system, another guaranteeing a stable military balance in Europe, and a political agreement (the Charter of Paris) in which every state subscribed to common ideals of democratic governance and free markets. Again, however, the Asian story was quite different.

The Cold War in Asia had acquired a character all its own from 1950 onward, when China went to war against the United States in Korea. From then on, the Cold War always had a different rhythm in Asia, with China usually holding the strategic initiative.[3] So the Cold War in Asia sometimes ran hot, even when the Soviets preferred caution (the Taiwan Strait crises of 1954 and 1958). It cooled when China was preoccupied with domestic concerns, even while the Soviets were triggering their own crises over Berlin and Cuba (1958–62). It heated up again as China prepared for renewed war against the United States (especially over Vietnam), even at a time when the Soviets wanted to avoid any such conflict. Then China turned its attention to revolution at home and the Soviet threat, as Moscow took over the job of being Hanoi's prime sponsor. As the Cold War was heating up again in the Third World and then in Europe, the Cold War in Asia had wound down. It was over by 1976, an outcome sealed by the result of the struggle over who would succeed Mao. But the Cold War in Asia ended with an armistice, not a peace treaty. There was never a real political settlement comparable to that in Europe.

In Europe, great power war is now hard to imagine, but in Asia, it is not so hard. The equilibrium in Asia is less stable, and the security institutions in place to preserve the peace are more fragile. So Asia really is different, and distinctive, and so is U.S. policy toward that region.

---

3. A country has the strategic initiative if it can effectively determine the time, place, and parameters (such as level of force) of a confrontation or conflict. China had this initiative in confrontations over Taiwan, India, and Vietnam (where its aid, commitments, and threats decisively influenced both the momentum of North Vietnamese moves and the constraints on the U.S. response, at least until 1969). For evidence, see Qiang Zhai, *China and the Vietnam Wars, 1950–1975* (Chapel Hill: University of North Carolina Press, 2000).

The Character of U.S. Engagement

The differences between U.S. policies toward Asia and U.S. policies toward Europe have been evident for a very long time. Six features stand out.

First, for at least a hundred years the United States has been intensely interested in its conception of order in Asia, especially Northeast Asia. The U.S. government cares about what happens, and often has a strong opinion. These opinions are not always welcome in the region, of course. But, just as in 1900, the United States presents the countries of Asia with a very tempting combination of interest, power, and *distance*. No other country's opinions come with such an appealing combination. So Asian countries tend to accept this American concern as legitimate and useful.

Second, U.S. interest in Asia has included a repeated willingness to spend political capital and commit armed forces. The United States fought two hot wars during the Cold War: both were in Asia. Moreover, the United States has occupied Japan. It has fought China, threatening Beijing on more than one occasion with possible use of nuclear weapons. It has fought North Korea and Vietnam. It has intervened actively in the internal political and military development of the Philippines, South Korea, Thailand, Indonesia, and Taiwan.

Third, the U.S. conception of order in Asia certainly excludes hegemonic dominion by another power. Although so far Japan and China are the notable candidates for this role, it is also worth recalling that the United States strenuously urged Britain, France, and the Netherlands to disgorge their imperial possessions in Asia, to the great irritation of those governments.

Fourth, for a century the United States has also been wedded to open economies and open trading opportunities in Asia (one of its old arguments with Britain). This has not been a simple story of good American free traders versus bad foreign protectionists: the United States has indulged in a good deal of protectionism in its own trading practices (as Australians know too well). However, the General Agreement on Tariffs and Trade (GATT) order, which was powerfully shaped by the influential bargaining of the British Commonwealth countries anxious to protect their preferences, succeeded because it allowed a good deal of economic nationalism. GATT thrived because it was flexible, and because it facilitated reciprocal movement toward a liberal economic goal. Above all, it succeeded because politics, not economics, compelled compromise. Economic cooperation in the free world seemed vital during the Cold War, and that political environment sustained GATT.

Fifth, the United States is nonetheless often erratic in the way it defines and defends its interests in Asia. To a greater degree than policies toward Europe or Latin America, policies toward Asia are likely to be top-down, driven by a narrow group of decision-makers. Few Americans had heard of Korea or Vietnam before their sons were asked to fight for those places. Guided from the top, the policies are more likely to fluctuate as circumstances change and constellations of concerned officials shift. In 1948, Washington decided not to intervene militarily in China's civil war. Two years later, the United States decided to defend Taiwan. In 1949 the U.S. government determined that it would not fight for Korea. The next year, when hypothetical problem turned to real case, this decision was reversed. In 1961, the United States agreed to the face-saving neutralization of Laos but, in 1964–65, scorned that option as a solution for Vietnam. In 1977, President Carter was utterly determined to withdraw U.S. ground troops from South Korea. By 1979, the White House had grudgingly changed its mind, an outcome that in hindsight seems very fortunate indeed.

In 1995, the United States, reading the Taiwan Relations Act (TRA) narrowly, reacted passively to Chinese missile firings in the Taiwan Strait. In 1996, however, when China escalated, the U.S. government chose to read the Taiwan Relations Act quite broadly, interpreting it as a pledge to defend Taiwan.[4] China was understandably surprised. The

---

4. Under the Taiwan Relations Act of 1979, any effort to determine the future of Taiwan by other than peaceful means is deemed "a threat to the peace and security of the Western Pacific area and of grave concern to the United States." On March 7, 1996, National Security Advisor Anthony Lake warned the Chinese deputy foreign minister that any action against Taiwan threatened the vital interests of the United States and would have "grave consequences" for China. This went beyond the TRA language. Lake's staff had researched the matter and Lake knew that no such warning had been issued to China about Taiwan since the original Nixon opening to China. Ashton B. Carter and William J. Perry, *Preventive Defense: A New Security Strategy for America* (Washing-

1996 decision may well also have been fortunate, since some evidence suggests that continued U.S. passivity might have encouraged the Chinese to proceed with invading one or more of Taiwan's offshore islands, for which they had already massed the needed forces.

U.S. reactions have been even more erratic in areas of especially acute interest to Australia, such as Southeast Asia. The U.S. ambivalence in 1999 during the East Timor crisis was obvious. Less obvious was the U.S. hesitation about adopting any active policy, other than economic remedies put together by the Treasury Department, in order to address the political unrest in Indonesia set off by the cascading economic crisis of 1997.

A sixth and final aspect of U.S. engagement in East Asia is its growing loneliness. Other outside powers have largely disengaged. Earlier in the century Britain, Russia, Germany, and France were major outside players in the region's affairs. In a strategic sense, they are now mostly gone. Asian powers have not taken their place.

None of these six observations would be especially worrying if conditions in Asia were in a stable equilibrium. Unfortunately they are not. In the coming five years, the erratic character of U.S. policy toward Asia may again carry great risks. The East Asian crisis that became evident in 1997 has usually been treated mainly as an economic crisis. This has let Americans feel that they are insulated from developments

---

ton, D.C.: Brookings, 1999), p. 97; James Mann, *About Face* (New York: Knopf, 1999), p. 336. Lake's quoted language is from Mann's interview with Lake.

At the same March 1996 meeting, Defense Secretary William Perry told the Chinese visitor that: "You have underestimated the political will of [the] U.S. The U.S. has vital national security interests which these actions threaten. You have not taken adequate consideration of the correlation of forces in the region. The U.S. has more than enough military capability to protect its interests in the region and is prepared to demonstrate that." In private, the interagency team working on the crisis judged that a Chinese attack or blockade would probably require the United States to defend Taiwan "because," according to a journalist who interviewed a participant, "the word 'blockade' is used in the Taiwan Relations Act." (The actual wording of the TRA refers to "boycotts or embargoes.") Yoichi Funabashi, *Alliance Adrift* (New York: Council on Foreign Relations, 1999), pp. 361, 368. Perry's quoted language is from Funabashi's interview with Perry; the crisis team material is apparently from Funabashi's interview with National Security Council staffer Sandra Kristoff. See also Carter and Perry, *Preventive Defense*, pp. 92–99.

in East Asia as long as their own economy seems largely immune. This complacency is mistaken. The United States faces a greater, and more complex, set of policy challenges in East Asia than at any time in the nearly twenty-five years since the end of the Vietnam War.

The crisis has generally led Asian countries to become more nationalistic and inward-looking. Some perceive a cynical design by Westerners to take over Asian assets at low prices. Events have shattered the supposed "Asian model" of economic growth. As in the 1920s, the "Washington system" seems dominant in every sphere. As it did then, this opportunity creates the burden of symbolic accountability. Even more than before, the United States represents an economic and political model that is being tested.

In the 1930s, the Roosevelt administration was a weak manager of the system. Even apart from the better known political and military events of the 1930s, the economic precedents alone are suggestive. When the United States went off the gold standard in 1933, it sacrificed international cooperation and weakened America's friends in Japan in order to gain more flexibility for domestic recovery. The Silver Purchase Act of 1934 practically destroyed the foundation of China's currency and its economic stabilization, but again, Washington was concentrating on a domestic agenda. In this new century, U.S. leadership may be tested in different ways, perhaps on its commitment to an open trading system, perhaps at new flashpoints of confrontation.

In the U.S. alliance with Australia, two small but recent stories illustrate the difference between alliance management and alliance neglect. In 1989, the Australian prime minister announced his initiative for creating the Asia Pacific Economic Cooperation (APEC) forum. He did so without prior consultation with the United States, perhaps because he excluded the United States from the organization in his initial design. That oversight was remedied. The mess was cleaned up skillfully, and a repetition was avoided during the remaining tenure of the Australian and American administrations.

Ten years later, with new leaders in Washington and Canberra, the Australian prime minister announced his intention to send troops into East Timor, and sought U.S. military help. What followed was an open and embarrassing disagreement with a confused and divided U.S. government. Although the prime minister may have discussed the matter directly with President Clinton just beforehand in an impromptu way, there is no evidence that the Australian government had privately consulted Washington about its plans in greater depth, and it particularly failed to do so with the Defense Department, whose help it meant to solicit. No allies in good communication with each other would have choreographed such a display of mutual bewilderment. For its part, there is no sign that the U.S. government (and its embassy in Canberra) made any noticeable attempt to intervene in the obvious Australian deliberations, to suggest a preferred course of action, or at least to reduce the appearance of disharmony, before the Australian decision was announced.

These are modest warnings. If they are heeded, an old lesson can be relearned: relationships with allies deserve as much attention as relationships with enemies. They can go wrong among the best of friends, and sometimes especially among friends.[5] If, on the other hand, alliances are strengthened and work well, they can be cables that stabilize wayward governments, aligning divergent impulses into coordinated strategies for steering through the twisty waters that lie ahead.

---

5. The classic study of a 1962 blowup in Anglo-American relations has now been published with fresh commentary and explanation. Richard E. Neustadt, *Report to JFK: The Skybolt Crisis in Perspective* (Ithaca: Cornell University Press, 1999).

Chapter 3

The U.S.-Japan Alliance

Stuart Harris and Richard N. Cooper

In the almost fifty years since the U.S.-Japan Security Treaty (USJST) was signed in 1951, not only have international circumstances changed, but major changes have also taken place within the two countries themselves and in their near neighbors.[1] Originally, the alliance was a traditional security alliance, intended to protect Japan from Soviet communism (and to contain Japan). However, it stimulated, and for its endurance almost certainly required, the development of complex interdependence between Japan and the United States. That relationship is now broad-based, encompassing a range of common values, common interests, and political processes.

Revisions and extensions to the USJST and related security policies have been necessary to adjust to changing circumstances over the years. Further adjustments were made in the 1990s to meet the needs arising from the end of the Cold War, the experience of rapid political change, and increasing global interdependence. Japan's International Peace Cooperation Law of 1992, permitting Japanese participation in UN peacekeeping operations, reflected changes in Japanese thinking about collective security cooperation. An alliance review, initiated by Prime Minister Hosokawa in 1994 and released by Prime Minister Murayama in 1995, concluded that the alliance was indispensable to Japan's security and was the key to regional peace and security. The review resulted in the revised National Defense Program Outline. Also important was the 1995 "Nye Initiative," which refocused U.S. security policy toward Asia and affirmed U.S. intentions to maintain approximately 100,000 troops in Asia. These intentions were reaffirmed in the 1998 strategy report, which also emphasized the continuing need for

---

1. The 1951 Security Treaty between the United States of America and Japan was replaced in 1960 by the Treaty of Mutual Cooperation and Security between Japan and the United States of America.

the alliance.[2] Japan's 1998 agreement to join U.S. theater missile defense (TMD) research, and the Diet's passage in 1999 of legislation on the revised 1978 guidelines for Japan-U.S. defense cooperation, largely completed a major stage in the process of adjustment of the alliance relationship in the military security field.

The collapse of the Soviet threat has important implications for the U.S. alliance framework, including the U.S.-Japan alliance. To the extent that shared opposition to the Soviet Union provided the glue that kept the alliance together, the question arises whether the more general objective of providing regional stability is enough to overcome periodic bilateral tensions. A division of labor in the region between Japan and the United States emerged in the early post–Cold War period. Japan increasingly assumed active political as well as economic roles (including providing economic aid) in East Asia, both bilaterally and multilaterally, while the United States maintained its stabilizing and balancing role. This division of labor is presently hampered by Japan's economic stagnation and by China's rise, but is likely to reemerge.

The foreign policy implications of the removal of the global threat are large. Domestic factors have become more central in themselves and in shaping foreign policies. Economic security has risen much higher on the security agenda and foreign policy has moved away from a global bipolar focus. For Japan, foreign policy now relates largely to the Asia-Pacific region, which has started to encompass South Asia as a result of the nuclear tests of India and Pakistan. In this region, Japan was taking independent steps even during the Cold War, and it is where Japan now believes it is often inadequately consulted by the United States.

This chapter starts by considering the costs and benefits of the alliance for the United States and Japan, and how these have changed over postwar decades. The analysis goes beyond the direct bilateral costs and benefits. The alliance does not just provide for Japan's security; it is central to the U.S. global and regional role and commitment. This chapter uses the cost-and-benefit framework to foreshadow where

---

2. U.S. Department of Defense, *The United States Security Strategy for the East Asia–Pacific Region* (EASR 1995) (Washington, D.C.: U.S. Department of Defense, February 1995); U.S. Department of Defense, *The United States Security Strategy for the East Asia–Pacific Region* (EASR 1998) (Washington, D.C.: U.S. Department of Defense, November 1998).

differences on bilateral or regional issues could develop between the alliance partners in traditional areas of tension or potential new ones, including burden-sharing, U.S. military bases, defense cooperation guidelines, TMD, economic relations, China policy, Taiwan, the Korean peninsula, Russia, and multilateral activities. Such differences will not undercut the need for the alliance; arguments for its continuation are based on more than just institutional inertia. The alliance helps maintain what both countries regard as an acceptable regional status quo, and it hedges against an uncertain, if presently relatively benign, environment. Although this chapter reflects a somewhat less concerned view of the regional security situation than that elaborated in Chapter 1, it still sees the alliance as crucial for that situation to continue. Changes in the management of the alliance are needed, however, to ensure that the alliance remains viable as it enters the twenty-first century. The chapter therefore concludes with some concrete recommendations, focusing especially upon the next five years, but within a longer perspective of ten to fifteen years.

Alliance Costs and Benefits

To sustain a bilateral alliance, benefits must exceed costs for both parties, but it is difficult to define and measure alliance costs and benefits precisely. They include not just immediate security benefits or financial costs, but often more substantial social and political costs and benefits. The U.S.-Japan alliance, in its bilateral context, was always accepted as an asymmetrical treaty. Although based on "mutual cooperation and security," it was limited to the security of Japan and its territories. Yet it is not just a bilateral alliance; from the start, it was part of the U.S. regional and global alliance framework. The U.S.-Japan alliance, although initially formed in part as a reaction to the Korean War then under way, had a global perspective; Japan was an industrial center to be denied to Soviet communism. Now, the alliance underpins U.S. management of its international relations — and its power diffusion — both regionally and, given the importance of China and potentially Russia, also globally.

Assessing the costs and benefits of the public good of regional stability is difficult; they depend largely upon both parties' subjective judgments of their magnitude. Moreover, what to some is a benefit is to others a cost. In Japan, a lack of military flexibility is seen as a benefit by pacifists or anti-militarists, but as a cost by others who want Japan to be a "normal" country. Some strategic planners in the United States would see Japanese rearmament as a benefit, while to others it would be a cost. Such differences are reflected in public attitudes. Policymakers may judge the alliance to have net benefits, but unless the publics in the United States and in Japan broadly agree, or if they perceive alliance burdens being unfairly distributed, it will be difficult to maintain the alliance.

The indirect costs and benefits to the two parties are likely to bear little relation to the direct financial costs. In the past, among the benefits to Japan were reduced threats of attack, including nuclear attack, from the Soviet Union, and savings on military expenditure that would otherwise have been incurred by Japan to provide for its own security; these savings facilitated its economic recovery. Past benefits also included U.S. aid and access to U.S. technologies. Today, the benefits to Japan are mainly a stable region in which there is no strategic vacuum, assurance against any threat from North Korea (or China or Russia), and continuing access to U.S. military technology and intelligence.

The costs to Japan include its acceptance of the victor's bases on its territory long after the end of World War II. Bearing an increasing proportion of the financial costs has been less controversial than the increased social and political costs of the U.S. military presence in Japan. For a while, Japan was potentially a target in any Soviet-U.S. military conflict; alliance membership, however, facilitated acceptance of Japan in regional affairs earlier than would otherwise have been the case. Neither is now relevant, but Japan's growing military capability would be disturbing to its neighbors if it did not take place within the U.S. alliance. More broadly, costs to Japan include loss of autonomy on some political and strategic matters; this denies it the normal security attributes of a mature state, requires it sometimes to support U.S. positions contrary to its own preferences, and risks its entanglement in U.S. military ventures. For good or ill, the alliance has substantially shaped Japan's politics and its approach to foreign policy. Other countries often see Japan as reflecting policy immobilism. In practice it has followed a relatively active foreign policy, albeit within the constraints of the U.S. alliance. Despite its global trade and investment interests, its policy has been largely regionally based, and focused on economic and aid relations. The question, now, is how Japan's foreign policy will be affected by the different circumstances under which the alliance will now operate.

For U.S. policymakers, the initial benefits, apart from denying Japan to the Soviet Union and to communism, were the availability of strategically located bases in a stable environment, and help in containing Soviet regional influence. These gave the United States political and economic influence in the region. Moreover, the alliance permitted Japan's early entry into the ranks of U.S. strategic allies. For U.S. and regional public opinions, an added benefit was the containment of a country potentially seen as a military threat and which might otherwise, however reluctantly, have gone nuclear.

WHAT THE U.S. WANTS FROM THE ALLIANCE, AND HOW IT HAS CHANGED
Alliance costs and benefits have changed considerably since 1951 for both countries. Compared with the emphasis on Europe during the Cold War, the relative economic and strategic importance of the region has risen for the United States, with the economic development of the last two decades and, in the 1990s, U.S. domestic concerns over Chinese and North Korean development of weapons of mass destruction (WMD).

The public perception that the alliance is simply for the protection of Japan's security greatly understates the benefits to the United States of the alliance. The alliance remains important as long as the United States emphasizes global commitment, regional engagement, and forward deployment. The USJST is the most important U.S. alliance in Asia, providing a major U.S. military foothold in a geographically strategic location that has increased in significance since the closing of the U.S. bases in the Philippines. It is at present the only major forward base from which the United States can project regional power, as distinct from providing deterrence. It is critical to the U.S. position in Korea; central to the U.S. role in East Asia; and symbolic, for those in the Asian region, of the U.S. security commitment. It provides a logistics platform for U.S. interests in Taiwan, and an ultimate security insurance policy for Japan. It also provides assurance to the region that Japan is not able to be militarily aggressive, and public opinion polls indicate that it is seen in a similar light by a substantial proportion of Americans.

JAPAN'S APPROACH TO THE ALLIANCE, AND HOW IT HAS CHANGED

Japanese views of the alliance have changed substantially over the almost half-century of its existence. In the early post-Occupation period, the alliance was the major pillar of Japan's defense policy. Although it slowly built up its own defense capability, Japan gave priority to its largely market-oriented economic recovery and growth.

Japan's view gradually became more regional in focus, particularly following the early 1970s Nixon shocks, as it developed a degree of foreign policy autonomy. U.S. pressure led to an emerging regional security focus under Prime Minister Suzuki; this included a limited and largely symbolic commitment to sea-lane protection for 1000 nautical miles around Japan. The concept of "comprehensive security" was articulated by Prime Minister Ohira in 1980 and specified as policy in 1981 partly to counter the domestic furor over what had been termed a "military alliance" in Suzuki's discussions with President Reagan. Subsequently, Prime Minister Nakasone used U.S. pressure for a greater Japanese contribution to the alliance to strengthen Japan's defense posture. This was also a time of major tensions between Japan and the United States over trade, but these tensions were cushioned, given an adequately constructive Japanese economic response, by the dominant U.S. strategic interest.

Resentment in Japan in the economic field, already rising, rose further over economic battles with the new Clinton administration. Moreover, Japan's booming economy in the late 1980s and some economic weakness and uncertainty in the United States gave Japan considerable self-confidence, while doubts grew about U.S. ability and willingness to stay involved with Asia. Whether a U.S. military presence was still needed also came into question. While some argued for a Pacific globalism to "sustain and invigorate" U.S. policy toward Asia, others argued for diminishing the links with the United States. Such views gained some support, but the 1990–91 Gulf War reminded Japan that its interests were global and dependent upon the United States, even as the first signs of Japan's economic distress were emerging. Nevertheless, the idea of becoming a "normal country" gained currency, implying some greater involvement in security cooperation, albeit usually within a UN context as with peacekeeping.

In 1994, following the Gulf War recriminations and their importance in turning attention back to the alliance, erstwhile opponents of the alliance, the socialists, accepted the USJST when the leader of the Japanese Socialist Party, Murayama, was prime minister. Domestic support for the alliance remains strong. Moreover, the 1994 North Korea nuclear crisis, China's military modernization, the 1996 missile crisis between China and Taiwan, and Korean peninsula problems, including the North Korea missile firing, have prompted a shift back toward the United States, a more regional orientation, and calls for increased defense capabilities.

A rightward shift in Japanese politics has recently become evident, with the return of the Liberal Democratic Party (LDP) and the decline of the socialists. Although much of the nationalist far right is opposed to dependence on the United States, it is conservative governments that have strengthened the alliance. Some pacifists remain opposed to the United States because of its military approach to issues, but others support the U.S. alliance on the grounds that it constrains Japanese militarists. Such proposals as giving formal legal status to the Japanese flag and national anthem, seen by critics as militarist, were passed without much difficulty by the Diet. Nationalism will remain an important issue in Japan, but how much it will affect the alliance will in part depend upon how the alliance is managed in the future. It is likely to enhance interest in the alliance by Japan's neighbors, as a restraint on latent Japanese militarism.

Areas of Possible Future Differences

The alliance has been remarkably robust, surviving numerous tensions during its existence, which, at the time, seemed likely to undermine alliance durability. Similarly, it has survived differences between Japan and the United States in critical areas, in part due to effective alliance management. For example, Japan often expressed public support for U.S. military policies with which it differed: Vietnam, the Gulf, and Kosovo. Exceptions were the publicly aired economic disputes. Economic differences, in the early 1970s and mid-1990s, were perhaps the one area where the alliance was at risk. There are a number of areas in which differences could arise in the future. All need careful management, but none threaten the alliance if handled skillfully.

DEFENSE COOPERATION GUIDELINES

In May 1999, the Diet passed three bills which, together, make up the new defense cooperation guidelines. These provide for Japanese rear-area support for the United States in regional crises, including search and rescue operations; logistics support including the use of Japanese hospitals, ports, and airfields, and the provision of fuel and equipment; and the use of Japanese ships to evacuate Japanese citizens from conflict areas.

It is not clear how much the Japanese public supports — or understands — the new guidelines. It is widely accepted that specific action to revise the guidelines was triggered by the North Korea situation, although the rise of China and the questions emerging from Japan's response to the Gulf War were important background factors. Public opinion polls, however, are not very helpful in judging Japan's perceptions on the nature of threats, the appropriate role of Japan in responding within the alliance, and the extent of support for the guidelines.

The guidelines were passed after a debate that raised complex and politically sensitive issues but, with some accommodations, did not arouse a great deal of opposition. The debate reflected concerns over what activities Japan's Self-Defense Forces (SDF) could validly participate in, consistent with Article 9 of Japan's constitution, as well as the geographic coverage of the guidelines. The legislation appears to require prior approval of the Diet for deployment of the SDF. It is subject, however, to a qualification, "except in emergencies," that meant that opposition attempts to retain Diet control of SDF activities were defeated. The question of SDF participation in implementing international sanctions, however, was deferred.

Although the Diet debate reflected substantial differences of opinion, the traditional political divide over defense issues has diminished substantially; in particular, the Japan Socialist Party (now the Social Democratic Party) has lost much of its power. Pacifists and anti-militarists are still strong, however, as are the risk-averse, who believe that providing support for U.S. actions might motivate attacks on Japan.

The guidelines involve more than just administrative changes. They have worried Japan's usually mistrustful neighbors who, accustomed to an alliance-based regional status quo, are uncertain how the changes will affect them, or fear that they foreshadow additional, less welcome, changes. They may also further reduce Japan's defense decision-making autonomy, the extent revolving around the ambiguities in the application of the guidelines. The new guidelines, like the old, cover problems in the Asia-Pacific region. Whether the region covered includes Taiwan was deliberately left ambiguous; however, the guidelines expanded the scope of cooperation, providing for "cooperation in situations in areas surrounding Japan that will have an important influence on Japan's peace and security." Thus the area for cooperation is not geographical but situational. Such wording avoids a decision as to where and when "cooperation" will take place; moreover, it leaves unclear who ultimately decides. If the decision when and whether to cooperate is up to Japan, that creates uncertainty for the United States. If the decision rests with the United States, then Japan's autonomy is diminished.

This is unlikely to raise problems over the Korean peninsula. The major area of potential difference would be over Japan's response under the guidelines, should the United States be involved in conflict with China over Taiwan. There have been arguments within Japan over whether the guidelines cover Taiwan; major differences of opinion remain, and reluctance by local government authorities to accept their role under the guidelines in providing rear-area support persists. Although how any crisis might develop will shape the actual responses to it, a request for Japan's involvement in a U.S. conflict with China over Taiwan, such as minesweeping in a blockade of Taiwan, is likely to impose major strains on the alliance, in the United States as in Japan. A negative or qualified Japanese response would disappoint U.S. expectations, putting the alliance at risk, while a positive response would put Japan at risk of Chinese countermeasures, would be divisive within Japan, and would prompt public opposition to the alliance. Thus, while the guidelines seemed to ameliorate the burden-sharing problem and strengthen the alliance in difficult circumstances, they could lead to major differences between Japan and the United States and put the alliance under potentially damaging strain.

Questions are already being asked in the United States about whether the guidelines should be more broadly defined in the light of changing alliance circumstances. It may be necessary in time to develop the guidelines further. The next five years, however, should be a period of consolidation to ensure effective implementation of what is already in place.

BURDEN-SHARING

Assessing who should carry what burden depends not just on each party's assessment of its own costs and benefits, but also its assessment of the other's. Since these are likely to differ, tensions may be difficult to avoid. Although burden-sharing became an issue in the 1980s, how the costs and benefits should be shared has been implicitly, if not explicitly, at issue from the start. Since the peak of U.S. "Japan bashing" in the 1980s, the U.S. attitude toward Japan has improved, deflated by Japan's economic crisis and deflected by U.S. public concerns about China. A U.S. economic downturn, however, could revive U.S. dissatisfaction with Japan.

Emphasis in the United States on the asymmetrical aspect of the alliance — easily articulated as Japan's security being assured by the United States but Japan not helping the United States on regional or wider problems while maintaining a large economic imbalance — contributes to U.S. perceptions of Japan as a "free rider," and accounts for the periodic emergence of burden-sharing as a public issue. However, the direct financial burdens borne by each party, which were asymmetrical for much of the alliance's existence, are now more balanced. Japan now covers a large part of the non-salary, non-military operations costs of the U.S. presence in Japan (the value of Japan's financial contribution to U.S. costs is currently around $U.S. 5 billion a year). The bases "are far more valuable strategically and as a political anchor than the highly touted and more publicly appreciated financial host-nation support provided by the Japanese government."[3] Nevertheless, periodic somewhat ritualistic debates over the issue remain important for their political symbolism.

Yet there is an increasing focus on the non-financial costs, such as providing troops (or risking casualties) for collective efforts, as in the Gulf War. Japan's initial non-responsiveness in the Gulf War, especially given Japan's overwhelming dependence on oil from the Gulf, and

---

3. Paul Giarra, "U.S. Bases in Japan: Historical Background and Innovative Approaches to Maintaining Strategic Presence," in Michael Green and Patrick Cronin, eds., *The U.S.-Japan Alliance: Past, Present and Future* (New York: Council on Foreign Relations Press, 1999), pp. 114–138, at p. 114.

complaints over Japan's role in Asia's economic crisis, raised U.S. concerns that Japan does not contribute fairly to alliance interests. The Japanese argue that Japan is not "free riding" in its security relationship with the United States, but is rather pursuing mutual security objectives by non-military means.[4] The United States has, at times, credited Japan for the benefits of regional economic integration that it has stimulated, and recognized Japan's contribution to aid programs as regionally stabilizing. Most of Japan's $U.S. 9–10 billion annually of aid goes to Asia (in contrast to U.S. aid).[5] The United States has pressed Japan to impose some broader political conditions on its aid, and to extend these conditions to aid beyond the region.

Japan has recognized the potential political difficulties for the United States, whatever the realities, of a perceived asymmetry. It used the Gulf crisis to introduce domestic changes that would otherwise have been more difficult, such as facilitating Japan's recent involvement in peacekeeping (e.g., in Cambodia), and revising the defense cooperation guidelines. Given the damage that misperceptions about the balance of alliance costs and benefits can inflict, governments in both countries need to counter these misperceptions.

U.S. MILITARY BASES

There are five major U.S. bases or base complexes in Japan: three on Honshu, one on Kyushu, and one on Okinawa. The Okinawa base complex, until recent reductions, occupied almost 20 percent of Okinawa's main island. The domestic politics in Japan of the bases became especially contentious after the September 1995 rape by three marines of an Okinawan schoolgirl, but more recently the bases crisis has subsided, helped by the Clinton-Hashimoto summit of April 1996 and various related measures taken by the United States to return about one-fifth of the land previously used for the complex to the Okinawan

---

4. See Yoshihida Soeya, "Japan's Economic Security," in Stuart Harris and Andrew Mack, eds., *Asia-Pacific Security: The Economics-Politics Nexus* (Sydney and Concord, Mass.: Allen & Unwin; Paul and Co. Publishers Consortium, 1997).
5. According to OECD Development Assistance Committee figures, in 1997 Japan's overseas development assistance (ODA) was $U.S. 9.3 billion, of which around three-quarters went to the Asia-Pacific region. This was down from $U.S. 10 billion earlier in the decade. U.S. ODA in 1997 was $U.S. 6.9 billion, less than a billion of which went to the Asia-Pacific region.

community. This included an agreement over the reversion of the site of Futenma Air Station, a key U.S. military base in Okinawa, to Japanese civilian control, central to scaling down the overall U.S. military presence there. Also important were efforts by Japan's government to reduce the disproportionate impact of the U.S. presence on Okinawa by providing considerable financial aid, although it resisted other Okinawan demands.

Japanese public opposition could rise again, however, if any untoward event occurs to increase the political costs to Japan of the continued presence of U.S. bases on Japanese soil. Moreover, although a variety of interests are involved, Okinawa retains the sense that its people carry an undue share of the bases burden. Arrangements for a substitute heliport for Futenma on Okinawa have still to be completed.

Japan's host-nation support is an important element of burden-sharing in the bilateral relationship. The present agreement on financial costs expires in 2000, and is being renegotiated. Although improvements in some administrative aspects of host-nation support are possible, an argument being made in the bargaining is that changing economic circumstances have made it more difficult for Japan to provide support than in the past. Yet in a weak domestic economy, financing local expenditures for the Americans is helpful from a macroeconomic perspective. The bases, central to the alliance, remain an area of sensitivity and potential tension. While there are difficulties for both sides to address in the idea of integrating the bases with the SDF on Okinawa, this has been extensively done in mainland Japan, the prime exception being the Yokota Air Base. It should be pursued as an option in Okinawa.

THEATER MISSILE DEFENSE

Japan's participation in U.S. research on TMD is also, to a degree, a response to U.S. pressure for greater burden-sharing. Support in Japan's security community for such a system gained strength with the 1998 North Korean missile firing. While lower-tier missile defenses will be put in place for the U.S. bases in Japan, an upper-tier system would be needed by Japan to counter a missile of the Taepodong 2 type used by North Korea, and the main Japanese interest is in the Navy Theater Wide (NTW) sea-based upper-tier system. Nevertheless, assuming the system works, and is not prohibitively costly, whether Japan will deploy an upper-tier system is a question for the future, and probably beyond our five-year time scale.

TMD has disadvantages for Japan as well as advantages. These include concerns that pursuit of the upper-tier system will undermine the 1972 Anti–Ballistic Missile (ABM) Treaty that, for Japan, is an important arms control measure. They also include regional responses. Japan is sensitive not just to China's political response but to the potentially destabilizing regional effect of a buildup by China of its missile strength to counter a U.S. or Japan-based TMD system. That would not only be against Japan's interests but could also lead others in the region to respond, resulting in a missile-building spiral. China opposes upper-tier missile defenses in general, but some Chinese consider Japan's involvement particularly provocative (more because of historically-based suspicions than logic), on the grounds that it could provide a shield behind which Japan could become militarily aggressive. More importantly, Japan is sensitive to China's concern that ship-based systems could cover Taiwan. For this reason, among others, whether the system is mounted on U.S. or Japanese ships is important. While complex in terms of alliance relations — political and alliance symmetry — the advantage for regional stability lies with mounting the system on U.S. vessels based in Japan. It would in any case take many years, at best, for Japan to handle an upper-tier system without major U.S. input.

ECONOMIC RELATIONS

Trade disputes, whether or not rationally grounded, from time to time risk derailing the security relationship. Between trade frictions in the United States and frictions over bases in Japan, a vicious circle might arise, in which corrosive rhetoric and inexperienced political leadership cause the alliance to lose the general political support in both countries necessary for its vitality.

Japan's main source of identity has long been its economic success, but its recent economic crisis has raised fears of a compensating increase in nationalism. To some extent, however, the problem of economic competition between Japan and the United States has diminished, as the U.S. economy booms while Japan's economy faces the consequences of structural problems.

The United States and Japan together accounted in 1998 for 42 percent of world output. Japan is the second-largest purchaser of American exports, and the United States the largest destination for Japanese exports. Japan's dependence on the United States has largely been maintained over the last three decades, but today it depends on the U.S. economy less in one respect: whereas in the early 1960s Japan ran a current account deficit, drawing in capital mainly from the United States, by 1998 Japan was a huge supplier of capital to the rest of the world, much of it to the United States.

Trade remains vitally important for Japan, despite the relatively low share of foreign trade in Japan's economy (exports remained at 11 percent of gross domestic product [GDP] between 1965 and 1998). Japan imports over 90 percent of its energy requirements, most other raw materials, and much of its food, and in the 1990s it increased its imports of manufactured goods, mainly from Asian countries. Japan depends more than most countries on open and secure sea-lanes, especially those from the Persian Gulf, from which it gets an increasing share of its oil imports.

Continuing frictions between the United States and Japan arise from difficulties of access to Japan's markets. Successive American administrations have emphasized the imbalance of Japan's huge bilateral trade surplus with the United States, augmented in 1998 by a Japanese recession combined with a booming U.S. economy. The two issues — restricted market access and large bilateral imbalance — are different in character and in origin, although in political debate they are often mistakenly conjoined. Together they have occasionally made some Americans and their political representatives very hot under the collar. In a world of multilateral trade, bilateral imbalances are normal and no source for concern.[6] These pressures are more easily overcome when the global and U.S. economies are doing well. As the global economy experienced some difficulty in 1998, concerns emerged, for example, over U.S. steel imports from Japan and other Asian countries.

The American position on trade has merit, but also poses a dilemma. Despite the general floating of exchange rates among major currencies since 1973, Japan has intervened strongly on several occa-

---

6. Australia, for example, normally runs a trade surplus with Japan and a deficit with the United States.

sions, especially in 1986–88 and again in 1993–96, to inhibit appreciation of the yen, which would have made Japanese exports less competitive and foreign goods more competitive in Japan's domestic market. During the latter period, consequentially, Japan's official foreign exchange reserves rose from $62 billion to $207 billion. The dilemma arises because of structural rigidities in the Japanese economy, and the prospect that a sharp decline in export competitiveness, instead of improving the trade balance, would cause a recession, a development not in the interest of Japan's trading partners. Thus both Japan and its foreign well-wishers have an interest in a restructuring of the Japanese economy to make it more adaptable, especially with respect to foreign trade.

The Japanese government and some Japanese firms have begun to address structural weaknesses in Japan's financial system and corporate governance; in time the Japanese economy will return to health. It is unlikely, however, ever to see the rapid growth experienced in earlier decades, both because of a prospective long-term decline in population and because, at least in manufacturing, it is now generally at the technology frontier, with little room for further technological catch-up.

The future importance of these various pressures will depend upon economic circumstances in both countries and how much the China issue supervenes. Any future economic problems are less likely than in the past to be shielded by strategic needs. The need exists, therefore, for greater understanding of the benefits of the alliance. Yet emphasis in the public negotiations over trade works in the other direction. While public differences over trade are not totally avoidable, given the interests involved, they are magnified by the compartmentalizing of policy by both countries, which leads to neglect of broader interests.

The Region: or, What Will the Neighbors Think?

A major purpose of the alliance is to contribute to regional stability. It would be contrary to this purpose if strengthening the bilateral relationship proved destabilizing to the region at large. This bears centrally on the cost and benefit assessments of the regional responses to the alliance.

U.S.-CHINA-JAPAN

Japan's relationship with China is a crucial one, and Japan has exercised great care in its diplomacy toward China since the Occupation ended. It has generally not followed the U.S. approach, most notably in its muted response to the 1989 Tiananmen Square tragedy. In the longer term, although Japan is anxious about how China might develop, generally its fear is not that China would attack Japan. Its concerns are about China's possible breakup or about problems in the region were China to become aggressive. Many Japanese analysts, like their counterparts in Europe and the United States, see China's potential for trouble as largely dependent upon how the international community treats China, believing it important to avoid the temptation to treat China as outside the international system. Hence Japan pursues a less confrontational, more "internalizing," multilateral approach to China than that commonly taken by the United States.

Some tension emerged over U.S. criticisms in reaction to Japan's 1990s economic crisis, their public articulation at the 1998 Clinton-Jiang summit, and because President Clinton visited China without also visiting Japan. These incidents were probably less significant in themselves than some U.S. commentators suggest, although blunt U.S. criticisms of Japan's economic policies remain irritants. Consequently, how the United States handles its China relationship is critical to the alliance's future. This is acknowledged by Japan, but poses a dilemma for it. When U.S.-China relations are good, the region is more stable, Japan's preferred situation. Yet Japan worries that U.S. relations with China might supplant those with Japan. When U.S.-China relations are not good, Japan's relations with the United States are better, but Japan then worries about regional stability. There has been some thoughtful questioning in Japan about whether, in the long run, U.S.-China relations may become more important to the United States and therefore whether in the long run U.S. interest in maintaining the treaty will remain. For a period well beyond the next five years, however, this is unlikely to become a serious issue among U.S. leaders.

A stable Japan-China relationship is achievable and crucial to Japan and to the countries of the Asia-Pacific region. It is also central to U.S. interests. Just as U.S. relations with China should be sensitive to their effect on Japan, enhancing U.S. relations with Japan should avoid provoking China as it gradually integrates itself into the international community.

CHINA

China has lived with the USJST for more than four decades. While it accepts that sovereign countries are entitled to form alliances, just as China itself did with the Soviet Union, China's view of the USJST and its potential for damaging China's interests has varied and will continue to do so. Its views originally reflected its ideological links with the Soviet Union, and then the souring of those relations. China's acceptance of the alliance has also been affected by how Japan is seen within it; China's concern has increased as Japan has moved from a subordinate position to one that seems, to Chinese eyes, of greater equality with the United States. China worries about a breakdown in an alliance that restrains Japan's militarization, but it also worries about Japan accepting added security burdens within the alliance, in part because it could lead Japan to become militarily assertive and further undermine Article 9 of Japan's constitution. One prominent U.S. scholar notes that: "Most Chinese analysts fear almost any change in the U.S.-Japan alliance."[7] Moreover, Chinese analysts drew a connection between NATO enlargement and a U.S. official's statement (subsequently disavowed) that the new guidelines are the Asian version of NATO's eastward expansion.

Since the end of the Cold War, the purpose of the alliance is seen as ambiguous. "It is at best searching for targets and at worst aiming at China,"[8] claims one Chinese writer. China increasingly sees the alliance as a means of containing China and fostering Japanese power, and its attitude toward the alliance largely depends upon the state of China's relations with the United States. China is less concerned about the new defense guidelines as such than with how they affect Taiwan, the issue central to the China-Japan relationship, as to the U.S.-China link. Hence China's particular concern over TMD, which it regards as linked

---

7. Thomas Christensen, "China, the U.S.-Japan Alliance, and the Security Dilemma in East Asia," *International Security*, Vol. 23, No. 4 (Spring 1999), pp. 49–80, at p. 58.
8. Yu Bin, "Containing by Stealth: Chinese Views of and Policies Towards America's Alliances with Japan and Korea after the Cold War," Discussion Paper, Asia-Pacific Research Center, Stanford University, September 1999, p. 5.

to the issue of Taiwan rather than to a North Korean threat. A further Chinese anxiety is the growing power and influence of Japan's conservatives, which China believes to be strengthened by the alliance (even though some Japanese conservatives oppose the alliance).

China has frequently been portrayed as an economic behemoth, about to tower over the rest of East Asia and even the world in the not-too-distant future. Reality is much more prosaic: China has grown rapidly for two decades, and is undergoing a remarkable economic transformation, but it remains a poor country by world standards, and still faces formidable challenges in modernizing its economy. If China continues to grow as rapidly as the World Bank foresees is possible (although not assured), by 2015 China's economy will rival, perhaps exceed, France as the fourth largest national economy in the world. It would still be significantly smaller than Germany and Japan, and barely more than one-quarter the size of the United States.[9] Chinese people would, on average, be nearly three times richer than today, but still just reaching the global average.

Anti-Japanese sentiments in China are still high, and with them remains a lingering, if not always rational, fear of Japan: China's senior leaders were born in the 1920s and remember Japanese brutality between 1931 and 1945. Both countries have behaved clumsily in establishing close relations in recent years, although the next decade could bring some improvement in this regard, now that Japan has come to terms with Korea, at least officially, over past Japanese treatment of Koreans.

The Chinese political elite objects to U.S. "hegemony," and probably deep in their hearts its members feel that China should (and eventually will) be dominant in East Asia. In the meantime, China needs a peaceful and prospering international environment in which to implement its difficult internal modernization. During that long period, China will welcome U.S. reinforcement of Japan's constitutional restraints on military forces and of its renunciation of development and deployment of nuclear weapons. From China's perspective, Japan already has formidable military forces, qualified only by their limited capacity to project power beyond range of their land-based aircraft. While Japa-

---

9. Conversions of GDP here are made at market exchange rates, which are relevant for international relations and foreign economic intercourse.

nese forces are limited in their capacity, they are fully modern. Japan's defense budget, even at the officially declared level of less than one percent of GDP, nonetheless is approaching four times China's published defense budget. China is acutely aware that, even adjusting for the high wages paid to Japan's all-voluntary force (whereas China relies on low-paid conscripts), Japan has far more funds available for operations and procurement than China does.

China has another source of ambivalence about U.S. forces, especially naval forces, in East Asia: as China grows and develops, its dependence on foreign sources of supply will also increase. It has been estimated that China will import 5 million barrels of oil a day by 2015 (it was a small net exporter in the early 1990s), and most will come from the Middle East. Thus, China's interest in a stable Middle East and the security of its sea-lanes from the Persian Gulf will grow correspondingly. So long as the United States and Japan remain closely allied, the maintenance of open and secure sea-lanes, essential for Japan, is likely to be assured for China as well. China would probably rather have that security provided by the United States, operating in the Indian Ocean as well as the Western Pacific, than by Japan or even India. The U.S. ability to base its Seventh Fleet partly in Japan greatly facilitates that U.S. role.

THE KOREAN PENINSULA

Korea has been important to Japan's search for a more independent and active foreign policy, and it welcomed Japan's move to view the relationship with Korea on its intrinsic merits rather than as part of the alliance framework This was reinforced following Kim Dae-jung's 1999 visit to Tokyo, during which Korea received a formal apology from Japan for Korea's colonial experience. A major purpose of the USJST, especially the new guidelines, is to support the U.S. position on the Korean peninsula. In any outbreak of violence on the peninsula, Japan would expect to give rear-area support to U.S. efforts on behalf of South Korea, despite its own political problems arising from its North Korean minority population. (It would not, however, expect to provide combat support to the United States on the peninsula, which would in any case be unwelcome to South Korea.)

The North Korean economy has fallen into a desperate condition. Its largest donor, China, like its other neighbors, wants to preserve the unsatisfactory status quo in preference to several uncertain alternatives. As a result, a best guess is that there will be no significant change in conditions on the Korean peninsula during the coming five years, beyond whatever additional cooperation the United States, with help from China, can wheedle out of North Korea on questions of proliferation of weapons of mass destruction and the missiles to deliver them. Over a somewhat longer period, however, continuation is difficult to imagine: either there must be significant economic change in North Korea, with the implication of gradual relaxation of security tensions on the peninsula, or the North Korean system will collapse completely.

While economic interdependence between South Korea and Japan is substantial, and although some bilateral discussions are being increased, security relations between the two nations remain limited. South Korea is watchful and somewhat anxious over Japan's increasing military potential. Noting the new defense cooperation guidelines, South Korea stressed the need for close consultation regarding Korean sovereignty. More generally, South Korea, like North Korea, is opposed to any significant increase in Japanese power-projection capability.

Japan, to a degree, feels shut out of the decision-making processes on U.S. North Korean policy and has, along with Russia, pushed unsuccessfully for an enlargement of the Four-Party Talks. Some effort has been made, as a result of the Perry report, to bring Japan more effectively into the process through the Trilateral Coordination and Oversight Group (TCOG) referred to by Ralph Cossa and Alan Oxley in Chapter 4. Japan has moved to develop political relations with North Korea. This initially posed problems for the United States (and South Korea), which had sought better prior consultation. Consultation has improved; Japan is more cautious; and South Korea, with changed policies, is now more responsive to Japanese aims.

Japan would not welcome improved relations with North Korea that lacked security assurances. Public opinion hardened after the North Korean missile overshot Japanese airspace; this led Japan to question its own commitment to the Korean Peninsula Energy Development Organization (KEDO). Such an event could happen again.

Japan's interests in the north Pacific could conflict with those of the United States were U.S.-China relations to worsen. This could result from Japan's interest in energy cooperation with China, Russia, South Korea, North Korea (if possible), and energy-rich members of the

Commonwealth of Independent States such as Kazakhstan. Japan wants to diversify its supplies of oil and gas, and to ensure sufficient development of energy resources to match the growing regional demand. To engender stability in the north Pacific, it also seeks to enhance cooperative relations and economic interdependence generally. So far, however, concrete progress in energy development has been minimal.

Eventually, however, the military stalemate on the peninsula will disappear; when it does, the situation that has framed U.S.-Korean military cooperation and conditioned the U.S. approach to the U.S.-Japan alliance will be drastically altered. Whether tensions are significantly relaxed, or the current North Korean regime collapses, the justification for retaining the U.S. Eighth Army in Seoul will disappear. A total withdrawal of U.S. forces from South Korea would leave Japan as practically the only country in East Asia with a U.S. — or any foreign — military base on its soil. That might, in time, reduce Japan's willingness to act as host to U.S. forces, although anxiety about a unified Korea, and its possible nuclear weapons capabilities, will remain.

On the other hand, the complete departure of U.S. forces from Japan would leave many countries in the region, including Australia, uncomfortable. Korea would be extremely uneasy, as fears of a remilitarized Japan reignited. Consequently, as argued in Chapter 4, Korea would probably provide facilities for some U.S. forces even after military tensions disappeared along the demilitarized zone (DMZ), provided the Eighth Army were withdrawn from its highly conspicuous (and economically valuable) location. This would not happen overnight, however, and thus for at least a decade, and perhaps for much longer, it is reasonable to expect that Japan will not be the only Asian host to U.S. forces.

Even with this potential area of conflict removed, and whether or not the alliance with Korea stays in place, the U.S.-Japan alliance will remain important for both parties.

RUSSIA

Russia's elites are as ambivalent about the USJST as they are about Japan. Some fear Eurasian encirclement, with NATO in the west and the U.S. alliance structure in the east. Other Russian leaders, however, differentiate the West from the East. Although NATO expansion in

Europe was regarded as a threat to Russia's core interests, in Asia the United States was, for a time after the Soviet collapse, viewed as a guarantor of the status quo. In what for Russia is basically a multipolar region, Russia saw itself as a possible partner in providing regional stability, balancing an emergent and potentially threatening China and an uncertain Japan. Since then, however, as it came to feel squeezed and marginalized in Europe, Russia has moved closer to China, but it is uncomfortable facing an emerging China. Many Russian leaders therefore saw the USJST as a key element in the regional military situation. They also considered it useful in preventing a more independent, militarized Japan that might act contrary to Russia's regional interests.

Russia's support for the alliance system, however, is conditional and is influenced by what it regards as adverse developments in the 1990s. It is concerned over U.S. missile defenses, including TMD in the region, and it seeks assurances that the new U.S.-Japan guidelines in the USJST are not directed at Russia, especially the Russian Far East. More generally it believes that the United States wants to limit Russian influence in the Asia-Pacific, and cites as evidence the failure to add Russia to the Four-Party Talks.

Russia has long proposed multilateral regional security systems; one motive is to ensure that Russia is not ignored. It argues that the existing regional multilateral dialogue forums in which Russia participates actively, notably the ASEAN Regional Forum (ARF), do not compete with the bilateral alliance framework, but contribute as a regional security system supporting the status quo.

MULTILATERAL INSTITUTIONS
The extraordinary success and longevity of the U.S.-Japan alliance, an alliance between the world's two largest national economies, is especially notable in a region with little tradition of alliances. The tradition of multilateralism is even more limited, but it has become important for Japan's regional foreign policy. Japanese pacifists see it encouraging peaceful resolution of disputes, while others see it as a means of resisting intrusive or unfair U.S. initiatives. In economic institutions such as the World Trade Organization and the Asia Pacific Economic Cooperation (APEC) forum, financial institutions such as the Asian Development Bank and the Executive Meeting of East Asia and Pacific Central Banks, and security institutions such as the UN and ARF, Ja-

pan's position does not simply copy that of the United States. It also participates in ASEM (Asia-Europe Meeting), which excludes the United States. Similarly, Japan sees its involvement in multilateral institutions as encouraging the United States to resist its own unilateral tendencies and to participate in the management of common security issues in multilateral settings.

Some U.S. observers, including one-time Secretary of State James Baker, were initially apprehensive that Japan might opt for multilateralism to the exclusion of bilateral alliances. Gradually, however, the United States accepted that multilateral security cooperation and the alliance could be mutually supportive in strengthening regional stability, and that multilateralism could strengthen bilateral relationships, including those among alliance partners.

The regional push to multilateralism in the security field poses no threat to the alliance in the foreseeable future, given its lack of collective security processes and its limited influence in addressing the continuing problems of North Korea and Taiwan. To the extent that such processes involve the United States in discussions of regional matters, they should be seen as valuable supplementary consultation processes.

The Future of the Alliance

Especially important among the issues in the U.S.-Japan relationship that could emerge as problems and gradually erode support for the alliance are those linked to the operation of the new defense cooperation guidelines and TMD as they affect Taiwan. Both are hostage to events on the Korean peninsula and over Taiwan, and could emerge as alliance problems in the next five years. Provided these aspects are managed carefully, however, both parties are likely to continue to believe that alliance benefits outweigh alliance costs.

DIRECT JAPANESE BENEFITS

Japan's direct security threats have diminished in the short term, and possibly in the longer term as well. Hence, while the social and political costs of foreign bases have increased, Japan's security gains from the alliance appear to be decreasing. Yet Japan still sees the alliance contributing to peace and stability in the region as a whole, symbolizing Japan's participation in the western global order, and assuring against strategic uncertainty. Moreover, Japan continues to benefit from access to advanced U.S. military technology and U.S. intelligence. In considering its security concerns, as well as conflict on the Korean peninsula, Japan is sensitive to the possibility of a re-emergent Russia that, although unlikely in the next five years, is possible within a decade or so. Japan is also sensitive to the unpredictability of North Korea and the longer-term uncertainties of a China that is modernizing militarily and has a history of intimidation by show of force. Japan also frequently expresses concern about its absolute dependence on secure sea-lanes.

Were the alliance to collapse, Japan would face a costly military buildup. A further Japanese concern would be the likelihood that this would be matched by military buildups in neighboring countries, in North Asia but also in Southeast Asia, and by general regional rebalancing. This would adversely affect Japan regionally. Many in Japan would also see this as raising the risk of loss of civilian control of the military, such as Japan experienced in the 1930s.

DIRECT U.S. BENEFITS

If the United States withdrew militarily from the alliance, its costs, defined broadly, would almost certainly increase. The costs of forward deployment, although high, are presently substantially covered by local support costs. Given the current U.S. concept of forward defense, loss of the Japanese facilities would require alternative facilities elsewhere, or else a much larger fleet, both of which would be expensive.

The costs of not being deployed forward would also be high, short of a major change in the U.S. conception of its national interest. A major concern would be Japan's temptation to go nuclear in these circumstances, and a resulting proliferation of nuclear weapons throughout the region.

POLITICAL CHANGE

Successive Japanese leaders in recent years have demonstrated support for the alliance at the official level. Political hopefuls and mainstream elites seem to take a similar view. Japan is changing, however, and the question now is how it will change in the future, both economically and politically, and what that means, domestically and internationally, for the alliance. A significant development has been the passage of a bill in the Diet to examine the possibility of revising the constitution. Over the next five to ten years, this review will deal with many issues, and one will be Article 9. This does not necessarily mean that support for the alliance will be reduced; possibly it suggests the contrary. Yet, as Japan seeks slowly to do more in the international arena, more independently, differences may emerge between Japan and the United States. Japan may find its autonomy, already limited under the alliance, further constrained under the new guidelines. Mostly, however, what Japan means by being a "normal" country would not take it outside the alliance.

U.S. attitudes are also changing. Within the United States, arguments are put forward from time to time questioning the U.S. global commitment, including the Asian alliances. There is also a continuing concern that the commitment to Japan is unbalanced. We argue that it is less unbalanced than is commonly thought, and that the bases are critical to the U.S. concept of its own security, which involves a strong forward presence and regional commitment. While it remains part of the public belief, that sense of imbalance remains influential; nevertheless, there is strong support for the alliance system by both major U.S. presidential candidates.

Conclusion and Recommendations

Japan and the United States, the world's largest economies, have a historically unprecedented relationship. Although commercial competitors, they are strategic partners rather than rivals. Given effective alliance management by both sides, the USJST, which fundamentally underpins this strategic partnership, will almost certainly remain the centerpiece of U.S.-Japan security relations for the next five years, and most probably for at least the decade or more beyond.

This strategic security partnership derives from a particular history. A victorious United States imposed a generous and constructive occupation on its defeated enemy after World War II, and Japan provided passive support for the United States during its subsequent military engagements in Korea and Vietnam. Japan has had enormous economic success, Japanese people have become rich, and Japanese technology and manufacturing processes have become world-class. Despite its present, almost certainly transitory, economic difficulties, typical Japanese enjoy standards of living unimagined by previous generations.

Over time, those who experienced the war and the Occupation have given way to new leaders and publics in both countries who lack that experience. They take for granted a relationship that is not self-evident and needs nurturing. In addition, the increased preoccupation with domestic issues in both countries has important implications for alliance management, making preservation of public support for the alliance more difficult.

Strains and tensions are inevitable in any substantial bilateral relationship, U.S.-Japan relations not excepted. However, common interests, substantially shared values, and compatible political processes, as well as the wide range of non-security links, greatly buttress the relationship. In the changed international environment, the interests of both parties have changed, but both share an interest in avoiding regional conflict or the rise of an alternative dominant power. Yet shifts in power relationships and political capabilities will not easily be accommodated. Moreover, a risk exists that constant carping over particular issues will get out of control and people will lose sight of the larger benign picture. Statesmen in both countries need to manage the alliance to avoid this and to ensure that the alliance structure evolves smoothly over time to accommodate necessary change.

Consequently, alliance management needs to be flexible, to seek greater substantive Japanese participation in the consultation processes involved, and to recognize the great sensitivity of actions requiring regional support from allies. Japan is becoming more regionally oriented: to a degree, it sees itself as increasingly Asian and has carefully managed its relations with China, in particular. With this increased emphasis on regional matters, and with regional impacts more important to Japan than global impacts, prior consultation becomes more crucial. While institutional inertia on both sides will favor continuation of the alliance, U.S. institutional inertia in this context could be a problem in terms of insufficient flexibility.

Given the changed circumstances, the predominant security orientation of U.S. Asia policy, and the U.S. tendency to see Asia in a military-strategic framework but not a political framework (in contrast to Japan's comprehensive security) have become less appropriate. The alliances have made this orientation seem natural and the East Asia Strategy Reports have become the major U.S. regional policy statements. There is a need, however, to fit regional security issues into a broader framework that encompasses other political issues. These would include Japan's growing concern that U.S. actions on the Comprehensive Test Ban Treaty (CTBT) and, prospectively, on the ABM Treaty reflect a declining interest in nonproliferation. They would account for the fact that Japan, China, and the region now see security in a wider, more comprehensive sense. A political framework would also help with the second problem, which is that involving Japan in a U.S. conflict with China over Taiwan would put great and possibly decisive strain on the alliance.

Japan will find it easier to support the United States outside the region than within. Thus, it needs to be more ready to contribute effectively outside the region. In most cases within the region, given effective consultation, few substantial problems should arise. Taiwan, however, would pose major problems for Japan: the very idea of becoming involved in a war with China would be unthinkable to most Japanese. Neither would Japan's involvement necessarily help the United States, given the region's persistent suspicions of Japan.

The United States faces a dilemma: if it were to allow the Taiwan situation to reach a point where it had to intervene militarily against a Chinese attack provoked by Taiwanese action, and if it then insisted on Japan's active support, the situation could put the alliance at risk whether Japan declined or agreed. Either U.S. expectations would be frustrated, or internal opposition would arise in Japan. Thomas Christensen argues that in these circumstances the United States should not expect the Japanese to be involved, but should instead plan to exclude certain activities by Japan, just as the United States chose to forgo Israeli assistance in the Gulf War.[10] Japan's involvement would be likely to increase the chances of escalation, and while the China-U.S. relationship would likely recover relatively quickly, for Japan the existing bitterness would be exacerbated for decades.

The challenge is how, in the new circumstances, to maximize the essential contribution of the alliance while foreseeing problems that could undermine it. Our recommendations follow.

---

10. Christensen, "China, the U.S.-Japan Alliance, and the Security Dilemma in East Asia," pp. 69 n. 59, 74.

A MORE COMPREHENSIVE U.S. POLICY TOWARD ASIA IS NEEDED
The new U.S. administration should articulate a broad, integrated and
coherent U.S. foreign policy for the Asia-Pacific region. It should in-
corporate U.S. political and economic as well as strategic aims and intentions toward China and other powers in the region, and should
state clearly how the U.S.-Japan alliance contributes to these aims. This
should help reassure Japan of its central role in U.S. regional policy. It
should encourage greater sensitivity in the United States to the negative, often unintended, externalities associated with U.S. alliance policies, such as those that might arise from the defense cooperation
guidelines, theater missile defense, and aid to Japan for an intelligence
satellite network.

To ensure that the alliance contributes positively to regional peace
and stability, the new administration's approach will need to be sensitive and flexible in responding to the changed environment in which
the alliance operates.

U.S.-JAPAN ALLIANCE MANAGEMENT
The new U.S. administration should pursue a steady evolution of the
U.S.-Japan alliance rather than seek major changes. The alliance is in
reasonably good shape: significant adjustments have been made to it
recently in the light of changing circumstances, and major changes in
alliance arrangements are not needed. Specific efforts, however, should
be made to:

CONSOLIDATE SECURITY COOPERATION GUIDELINES. The new security
cooperation guidelines have been important in improving overall alliance relations. In the next few years at least, the U.S. and Japanese governments should concentrate on consolidating the new guidelines and
making their implementation effective rather than attempting to extend them.

IMPROVE PUBLIC SUPPORT FOR THE ALLIANCE IN BOTH JAPAN AND
THE UNITED STATES. The incoming U.S. administration should give
high priority to briefing the new Congress and the media on the benefits of the alliance relationship to the United States, as well as to Japan
and the region. In particular, emphasis needs to be given to explaining
the continuing relevance of the alliance despite the passing of the Cold
War. Moreover, to the extent possible, both governments should try to
limit official criticism of each other in their countries by periodically
reconciling public interests of the two countries across a broad field.

In the United States, the new administration should reduce existing compartmentalism in the presentation of various U.S. policies toward Japan and move toward a "whole of government" approach that would ensure that, on the U.S. side, proper weight is given to broad alliance interests. The process of negotiating in public in the economic arena (and over host-nation support) that such compartmentalism encourages has a negative public effect that lasts beyond the end of the negotiations.

The new U.S. administration should also recognize the importance to Japan, and to public Japanese support for the alliance, of international arms control and nonproliferation endeavors, and the impact on these that Japan fears if the introduction of upper-tier TMD in the region seemed to jeopardize the ABM Treaty.

DO NOT HARM JAPAN-CHINA TIES. The fall of the Soviet Union has in one respect reduced the intensity of the U.S. need for an alliance with Japan. The continuing shift of economic power to the Asia-Pacific region, however, and U.S. differences with China, greatly accentuated by domestic U.S. congressional politics, mean that U.S. security interest in the region will remain, even were the North Korean problem resolved. Since the alliance system should contribute to regional peace and stability, the new administration should seek to ensure that changes in the alliance do not add uncertainty to the region. In particular, the alliance should not adversely affect Japan-China ties. This should include not pressing for support within the alliance that would cause undue regional or domestic resentments that outweigh any benefits from the support.

Since a major regional concern must be the trilateral relationship between China, Japan, and the United States, the new U.S. administration should continue efforts to establish a trilateral (U.S., Japan, China) or quadrilateral (to include South Korea) discussion process, perhaps as an adjunct to the APEC leaders' meeting.

ENHANCE BILATERAL CONSULTATIONS. Differences will inevitably emerge between Japan and the United States in their approaches to the region. The new administration should ensure that effective consultation processes are in place that give Japan a voice in alliance policy before decisions are actually made. This may involve new processes and mechanisms. Given Japan's links with the region, this could benefit policy decision-making.

The United States and Japan should continue and extend their existing bilateral discussions on regional issues with other major regional countries. Enhanced bilateral consultations should take place among alliance partners, but it would be counterproductive to seek to extend this to any kind of coordinated security partnership among the alliance partners.

GIVE DUE WEIGHT TO BENEFITS IN ASSESSING BURDEN-SHARING. The new administration's approach to burden-sharing should be based on a recognition that the strategic and political value of the bases to the United States is central to the U.S. global and regional commitments, as well as beneficial to Japan.

ENCOURAGE SENSITIVITY TO THE MILITARY BASES ISSUE IN JAPAN. In Okinawa, as elsewhere in Japan, the new administration needs to be sensitive to the genuine, as distinct from the politically based, concerns in Japan over the U.S. bases. To ameliorate the real concerns and to counter the politically expedient opposition, the option should be offered to the SDF to integrate with the United States in the operation of the U.S. military bases.

LIMIT TMD TO U.S. SHIPS. Upper-tier TMD is a step with important implications for Japan and the region. For the sustainability of the alliance and for regional stability, the new administration should ensure that, should sea-borne upper-tier TMD be introduced, it should, at least initially, be mounted on U.S. ships based in Japan.

MANAGE ECONOMIC RELATIONS. Given that periodic tensions will be likely between Japan and the United States in economic fields, it will be important to keep such differences to manageable proportions. While even unbalanced economic exchange can be a positive-sum game, the new administration, along with Japan's government, should work to reduce the adverse external effects of raucous public exchanges over small differences by improving coordination of U.S.-Japan diplomacy.

To prevent drift in the relationship, and extended U.S. public and Congressional criticisms, Japan, as part of its regional leadership role, should be more forthcoming in eliminating its remaining restrictions in the economic field on trade and its remaining barriers to foreign investment, to make investment in Japan more attractive internationally.

Chapter 4

The U.S.-Korea Alliance

Ralph A. Cossa and Alan Oxley

While the rest of the world struggles to develop new post–Cold War (or post post–Cold War) paradigms, on the Korean peninsula vestiges of the era of containment still linger. Fifty years after the initiation of one of the first and bloodiest battles of the Cold War and some forty-seven years after the initiation of what now constitutes the world's longest-running armistice, the immediate purpose of the 1954 Mutual Security Agreement between the Republic of Korea (ROK or South Korea) and the United States remains clear and consistent: to deter aggression from the Democratic People's Republic of Korea (DPRK or North Korea).

This chapter addresses the current state of the U.S.-ROK alliance and efforts both to preserve peace and to bring about the eventual reunification of the peninsula. It also takes a look out five years to describe the trends and challenges that will affect progress toward these goals. It concludes with recommendations on how to manage the alliance until reunification is achieved, and beyond.

Current Security Environment

One of the major foreign policy challenges facing the United States and the ROK today is managing their relations with a potentially volatile and generally unpredictable (and unappreciative) North Korea. This has both deterrent and diplomatic components.

The threat from North Korea remains real, if somewhat diminished as a result of North Korea's economic bankruptcy, its dwindling military capabilities relative to the South, and the adjustment of its Cold War alliances that previously provided less restrictive security assurances. Despite these changes, "North Korea is still capable of inflicting terrible destruction on South Korea, especially with artillery, missiles, and chemical weapons."[1]

Economic and social hardships notwithstanding, the size of the North Korean military has not been diminished; rather it has experienced slight growth in overall numbers and in new hardware over the past decade. North Korea possesses one of the five largest armed forces in the world, with some 1.2 million active duty military personnel armed with over 4,000 tanks and 10,000 field artillery pieces. One-fourth of North Korea's population, some five million men and women, serve in the reserve forces. With 65 percent of its forces heavily fortified and situated in close proximity to the demilitarized zone (which itself is less than 25 miles from Seoul), the first few days of a North Korean–initiated conflict would be extremely destructive.

Pyongyang's ability to sustain combat against the South is suspect, however, due to doubts about its logistics, ammunition and fuel stockpiles, and questionable support from its long-standing allies. Both Moscow and Beijing have made it clear in recent years that their security relationships with Pyongyang do not guarantee support if Pyongyang were to instigate a conflict. Most military analysts agree that a North Korean invasion of the South, while initially very damaging, would ultimately end in the destruction of the North Korean state.

The principal deterrent to North Korean aggression continues to be South Korea's well-equipped, highly capable, well-trained 672,000 military forces, further augmented through its alliance with the United States. The 37,000 U.S. military forces on the peninsula serve as a symbol of U.S. commitment and as a "tripwire," ensuring that the United States will become fully engaged immediately upon the initiation of hostilities by the North. U.S. forces would quickly swell to over 500,000.

Lending further credibility to this deterrence capability is the U.S./ROK Combined Forces Command (CFC) that evolved from the multinational United Nations Command (UNC). The UN Command, which includes representatives from the United States, ROK, Australia, and fourteen other countries, oversees the 1953 Armistice. The CFC was established in 1978 in order to give the ROK a greater role in the

---

1. U.S. Department of Defense, *The United States Security Strategy for the East Asia–Pacific Region* (EASR 1995) (Washington, D.C.: U.S. Department of Defense, February 1995), p. 24.

war-fighting planning and command structure. The establishment of the CFC was part of a bilateral agreement calling for a U.S. transition "from a leading to a supporting role" in the defense of the peninsula, to ensure that the ROK military had a greater role in the operational planning and combat command and control of combined ROK/U.S. forces during peacetime and in the event of hostilities.

While the CFC structure allows both for a smooth transition from peace to war and for an effective combined war-fighting effort, many in the ROK continue to call for greater indigenous operational control of ROK military forces. Such issues play to the South's "little brother" complex, an irritant which must constantly be addressed. They do not detract, however, from the deterrent value of the alliance or its centrality to broader ROK-U.S. relations.

Deterrence has continued to work, even as U.S. forces were engaged elsewhere (Vietnam, the Persian Gulf, Kosovo). This does not, however, allay the concerns laid out by Paul Dibb elsewhere in this volume about the U.S. ability to conduct two major regional contingencies simultaneously, should deterrence fail. The United States would, in fact, be hard pressed to fight decisively on the Korean peninsula while involved in another Desert Storm–type contingency elsewhere unless it resorted to its wide arsenal of tactical or strategic nuclear weapons. This disturbing but nonetheless real possibility, while not openly discussed, no doubt has a deterrent value of its own.

Current Diplomatic Efforts

Several core diplomatic initiatives currently guide U.S. and ROK policy toward the North. First is the October 1994 "Agreed Framework Between the United States of America and the Democratic People's Republic of Korea," under which Pyongyang agreed to freeze its current nuclear research program in exchange for interim U.S. heavy fuel oil deliveries and the eventual construction of two nuclear-energy light water reactors (LWRs). For better or worse, the Agreed Framework lies at the heart of current U.S. strategy for peace on the peninsula. While the Agreed Framework has come under increased criticism as a result of both real and suspected North Korean misbehavior, the United

States and its allies and North Korea, even today, remain better off with the Agreed Framework than without it.[2]

Most significantly, the DPRK's suspected nuclear weapons program at Yongbyon remains frozen and Pyongyang has allowed for the canning and continued safeguarding of the spent fuel of the DPRK's existing reactor by the International Atomic Energy Agency (IAEA). This, in and of itself, is a major contribution to U.S. non-proliferation goals. The Agreed Framework also provides a vehicle for dialogue and a standard by which to measure DPRK sincerity and willingness to cooperate. For example, during the 1999 standoff between Washington and Seoul over Kumchangri, a suspicious North Korean underground facility that was believed to be nuclear-related (in violation of the Agreed Framework), the North was willing to submit the site to U.S. inspection rather than let the Agreed Framework die, even if it could not resist using tried and true brinkmanship techniques to gain additional benefits before relenting to an inspection.

The Agreed Framework does not provide the North with a free ride. It ties ultimate success — and the provision of key LWR components — to specific future DPRK performance. The North must continue to cooperate and become progressively more transparent in order eventually to obtain the two light water reactors.

The second diplomatic initiative is the Korean Peninsula Energy Development Organization (KEDO), created by the United States, ROK, and Japan to implement the Agreed Framework. Through KEDO's efforts, the United States has thus far accomplished its two primary Agreed Framework obligations: arranging for fuel oil deliveries and undertaking construction of the LWRs. KEDO has also become an important vehicle for direct South-North contact. KEDO has transformed the bilateral U.S.-DPRK Agreed Framework process into a multilateral effort in which the Republic of Korea now plays a leading role. This has also helped restore South Korean confidence in the United States, confidence that was shaken during the negotiating process leading up to the Agreed Framework.

Another diplomatic effort is the Four-Party Talks, a series of formal talks among North and South Korea, China, and the United States

---

2. For a line-by-line assessment, see Ralph A. Cossa, *The Agreed Framework: Is it Still Viable? Is it Enough?* (Honolulu: Pacific Forum CSIS Occasional Paper, April 1999).

aimed at replacing the July 27, 1953, Armistice with a formal peace treaty. While the Talks have not made much substantive progress, their mere existence achieves several important purposes. The Four-Party Talks reiterate to North Korea that a separate peace treaty with the United States that excludes the ROK remains out of the question; underscore the commitment of the other three parties to the armistice until such time as a treaty is achieved; keep Pyongyang engaged in a give-and-take dialogue process; offer an opportunity for direct discussions between North and South; and provide China an opportunity to be actively involved in the peninsula peacemaking process.

Fourth is ROK President Kim Dae-jung's policy of "Constructive Engagement" with North Korea (more commonly referred to as the "Sunshine Policy"), which provides the broad framework and operating principles through which Seoul manages its own relations with Pyongyang. This long-term, comprehensive strategy embraces both cooperation and deterrence. Its declared principles are that South Korea "will not tolerate armed provocations of any kind," "does not intend to absorb North Korea," and that it "will actively promote exchanges and cooperation between South and North Korea."[3]

This is a politically courageous long-term policy that is more widely than deeply supported within the ROK. Even minor acts of provocation by North Korea cause opposition politicians to heap scorn upon President Kim's approach to the North; many even within his administration and in the broader security community who pay lip service to the policy openly question whether it is too trusting or optimistic in dealing with Pyongyang.

The Sunshine Policy calls for a gradual opening up of the North and confidence-building measures to pave the way for eventual reunification. The main difference between this policy and earlier approaches is that it accepts allowing the North to die of natural causes, rather than trying to hasten its demise by prematurely turning off life-support systems. It is premised on the idea that a great deal of "stage setting" must occur before the two sides can even seriously think of merging. This is meant to diminish the North Korean regime's sense of threat, making it more inclined to cooperate, and less likely to lash out in irrational ways.

---

3. "President Kim Dae-jung Commemorates 50th Anniversary of the Republic of Korea," *Korea Update*, Vol. 9, No. 6 (August 15, 1998), p. 4.

The last and perhaps most influential diplomatic effort is the so-called "Perry Initiative" — the State Department's October 1999 "Review of United States Policy Toward North Korea: Findings and Recommendations" prepared by former Secretary of Defense William Perry — which seeks to tie all the disparate elements of U.S. policy toward North Korea into one unified, closely-coordinated package. Perry lays out two paths for future U.S.-DPRK interaction: enhanced cooperation or enhanced deterrence. The decision as to which path to take will be dictated by North Korean behavior.

Perry has also managed to facilitate greater three-way cooperation among Seoul, Tokyo, and Washington through the creation of an institutionalized framework, the Trilateral Coordination and Oversight Group (TCOG). While the extent of cooperation and degree of harmony may at times be overstated, there is no question that, through the TCOG process, the three countries have more successfully managed their somewhat differing views on the potentially contentious issue of how best to deal with North Korea.

The Initiative's firm, unified carrot-and-stick approach contributed greatly to North Korea's willingness to refrain from destabilizing actions, and specifically to its agreement to refrain from long-range missile testing in return for a partial lifting of U.S. economic sanctions. North Korea had previously argued, with some justification, that the U.S. refusal to lift sanctions put the United States in violation of the Agreed Framework. Pyongyang's decision to cooperate on missile testing makes further progress in its relations with Washington and Tokyo possible. It also removes a potential irritant in U.S.-ROK and U.S.-Japan relations, while keeping South Korea's Sunshine Policy of increased engagement with the North alive.

Perry's report represents a significant step forward in the development of a comprehensive, coordinated strategy, but it remains to be seen just how vigorously current and future U.S. administrations will pursue his recommendations, and whether the North Koreans will choose the right path. The United States is still a long way from crafting a bipartisan long-term strategy toward North Korea, but the Perry Initiative at least provides a starting point. It also puts the three key allies on the same sheet of music. These are no small accomplishments, but they are not enough; below, in the recommendations section of this chapter, Perry's suggestions are viewed and placed in broader perspective.

One positive outgrowth of the Perry report is the current freeze in missile testing. The launch of a North Korean three-stage rocket on August 31, 1998, in what is generally believed to have been an unsuccessful attempt at a satellite launch, increased U.S. awareness and concern about North Korea's missile program. Since portions of the rocket flew over Japan, it also prompted Japan to withhold its promised funding for KEDO for several months. While Japan has since agreed to resume its financial support to KEDO, Japanese officials have declared that another missile firing over Japan will result in an immediate termination of Japanese contributions toward the funding of North Korea's light water reactors. It would also provide additional ammunition to those in the U.S. Congress who want to see a much harsher policy toward North Korea. At a minimum, another test would further restrict, if not kill, future Congressional funding of KEDO and any North Korea–related assistance programs. Most importantly, it would be seen as a North Korean rejection of the Perry invitation to travel down the path of enhanced cooperation.

Even if missile tests remain halted, North Korea's missile development efforts and its indiscriminate willingness to sell missile hardware and technology continue to raise both security and political concerns. The U.S. Congress has tied future funding for KEDO to Clinton administration efforts to halt North Korea's missile development and export programs. Thus, while the Agreed Framework was never intended to address North Korea's missile programs, the two have become inextricably linked.

For its part, North Korea claims that it has a "legitimate right of self-defense to develop, test, and produce missiles," especially given the threat posed to it by the U.S. missile and nuclear arsenals. But DPRK negotiators are quick to add that they are willing to discuss an end to their export of missiles and related technology if handsomely compensated; the North has reportedly asked for up to $U.S. 3 billion to halt its missile sales. Pyongyang is not likely ever to give up completely what it sees as both an ace in the hole and an invaluable insurance policy.

Looking Toward the Future

Pundits as recently as 1998 were predicting that North Korea was heading toward an imminent collapse; the odds were high that the leadership in Pyongyang would not be around to witness the new millennium. Nonetheless, North Korea remains alive and kicking (if not necessarily very well), and the conventional wisdom is now that it will continue to muddle through. Likewise, just before the Asian crisis hit in earnest in late 1997, most were still hailing the ROK's economic miracle as unstoppable. Few predicted the dramatic collapse of Seoul's economy and even fewer its (thus far) rapid recovery.

An attempt is made here, nevertheless, to forecast the most likely and most desirable future five years hence, as a basis for recommended policy options that might help increase the likelihood that the most desired outcomes will be achieved.

There is one basic assumption upon which the following recommendations rest, namely, that current U.S. alliance-based strategy toward maintaining peace and stability in the Asia-Pacific — anchored on long-standing U.S. security relationships with Canberra, Tokyo, and Seoul — will continue over the next five years (albeit with some modifications and adjustments, perhaps including those recommended in this volume). This entails a continued, credible forward U.S. military presence based in Korea and Japan (and more modestly in Singapore), and a continued multinational security guarantee involving U.S. and Australian forces (among others) under the UN flag on the Korean peninsula. From this basic assumption flow the following predictions.

THE DPRK WILL SURVIVE
The odds are high that North Korea will still exist as a separate nation five years into the new millennium. This does not necessarily mean that the current regime will still be in power, although Kim Jong-il's staying power should not be underestimated. Should Kim die, of natural causes or otherwise, he will most likely be replaced by someone in the current North Korean hierarchy. Various heirs-apparent (or not so apparent) are probably being groomed, if not in senior political or military circles in Pyongyang, then perhaps in Beijing or elsewhere.

While the most desirable circumstance five years hence would be a peacefully reunified peninsula under Seoul, there is no credible scenario to get there from here. A collapse of the current regime is more likely to result in another communist regime taking its place. It may be designed more along the lines of the current Chinese model than the inflexible model being followed by the North today, but it will still be composed of leaders who are not ready to abandon the North's system or permit full integration with the South. Asking the current regime to take the full integration path is equivalent to asking them to commit suicide, and this remains improbable.

Thus a new regime or a somewhat more cooperative Kim Jong-il regime — that is, one inclined to follow the Chinese model of economic reform — appear the best that can be hoped for. From the U.S. and ROK perspectives, this is not all that bad, given the enormous costs that would be involved in full integration at this stage of the game. Regardless of who is in control in the North, regime (and personal) survival will remain the primary objective and this will dictate a cautious if not paranoid and contrarian approach toward Seoul and Washington.

WAR ON THE PENINSULA REMAINS UNLIKELY

If the alliance remains intact, it is unlikely that North Korea will launch an all-out invasion of the South during the next five years. Such an action would result in the total elimination of the North Korean state. While North Korea's leaders may appear unpredictable, survival remains their highest priority. More likely is continued provocation, by actions meant for reconnaissance and harassment more than a serious military threat against the South. One can also argue that North Korea requires a certain amount of tension and confrontation in order to justify its own separate identity (and its repressive political system). In short, while the North Korean leadership may act in generally unpredictable, provocative ways at the tactical level, they will likely remain cautious at the strategic level, understanding that their very survival is at stake.

TRUE PEACE REMAINS UNLIKELY

True peace remains unlikely, although the North will show more flexibility. A major breakthrough in South-North relations that is sufficient to result in a call for the end of the security alliance or the complete removal of U.S. forces from the peninsula is unlikely. However, modest tactical changes in the North's posture and bargaining position toward the South can be expected. The North seems to understand that Kim

Dae-jung's Sunshine Policy and the Perry Initiative are the best it can hope for, and that any subsequent policy initiatives, from the current or any future U.S. and ROK administrations, are likely to be much more restrictive. As a result, Pyongyang appears to be nibbling cautiously at the carrots being offered by Seoul and Washington.

A FORMAL PEACE TREATY WILL BE SIGNED

While current North Korean stonewalling makes the following prediction a bit bold, there is a better than even chance that there will be a South-North peace treaty before 2005 (and most likely before 2003). Kim Dae-jung's term is up in 2003 and he is constitutionally prohibited from running for a second consecutive term. While it is too soon to predict who might replace Kim Dae-jung, it is a safe bet that he or she will be less forthcoming and flexible toward Pyongyang unless the North makes some significant gestures in the next three years. The North could and should conclude that signing a peace treaty with Seoul during Kim Dae-jung's administration represents its last best chance of preserving regime and state survival.

A genuine, full rapprochement does not appear possible, however, at least not one characterized by open borders and greater freedom of movement and South-North interaction. The most likely future scenario is one in which North and South acknowledge each other's right to exist through the establishment of diplomatic relations.

By 2005, South-North relations are likely to be only in the early stages of the reunification process, similar to the situation between East and West Germany in the early 1970s around the time of the Helsinki Accords. The establishment of diplomatic relations between Washington and Pyongyang (and between Tokyo and Pyongyang) is also likely during the next five years; it could even precede South-North diplomatic relations, although it would be wiser to link these events.

A U.S. MILITARY FORCE PRESENCE WILL REMAIN

Even if the most optimistic forecasts are realized, such developments do not obviate the need for a continued U.S. military presence on the Korean peninsula. Logic dictates a continued presence of U.S. forces on the peninsula as long as North Korea exists. While a genuine reduction in tensions — along with further improvements in U.S. rapid deployment and power projection capabilities — could result in some modest drawdowns, a credible deterrent force under the current alliance structure will remain.

Nonetheless, if some level of rapprochement between North and South occurred, the pressure would be great on both Seoul and Washington over the next five years to significantly reduce (or eliminate) the U.S. military presence. Ironically, one of the biggest impediments to achieving a peace treaty is North Korean insistence at the Four-Party Talks that U.S. forces on the peninsula be put on the bargaining table, something Seoul and Washington (rightfully) refuse to consider. Yet, the one event (short of the dissolution of the DPRK) that would most put pressure on Washington and Seoul to rethink the issue of a U.S. military presence would be the signing of a peace treaty.

THE AGREED FRAMEWORK/KEDO PROCESS WILL CONTINUE

The fate of the Agreed Framework five years hence is difficult to predict. Given the delays, the original target year of 2003 will come and go without the completion of the LWR project. Even if everything goes without further hitches or delays — and the odds of that happening are very low — it appears unlikely the LWR project could be completed by 2005. There are too many moments of truth yet to come, most important among them a full accounting by North Korea to the IAEA of its past activities.

Although the two LWRs may not be fully delivered by 2005, the Agreed Framework process may continue. Future administrations in Washington and Seoul will have less vested interest in the Agreed Framework, but none will be eager to see it end precipitously, since this would be likely to result in a resumption of unchecked North Korean nuclear weapons research and development activity (including plutonium reprocessing). This in turn could trigger a potentially explosive showdown between Pyongyang and Washington, even drawing in the broader international community. As a result, continued engagement through the Agreed Framework/KEDO process appears likely, unless supplanted by more comprehensive mechanisms.

THE PRC WILL CONTINUE TO PROTEST AGAINST U.S. ALLIANCES AND FORWARD MILITARY PRESENCE

Five years from now, the PRC will be no more supportive of the U.S. bilateral alliance structure and forward military presence in Asia than it is today. There are fundamental differences between Beijing's vision of the peninsula's future and that espoused by President Kim (and pre-ferred by the United States). President Kim has stated repeatedly that he sees a post-reunification role for the U.S.-ROK alliance that includes a continued U.S. military presence on the peninsula. Chinese leaders would prefer a future Asia in which China and not the United States plays the primary regional balancer role, where military alliances ("leftovers from the Cold War") no longer exist, where a reunified Korea looks to Beijing for its security guarantees (perhaps against their common Japanese threat), and where U.S. military forces are no longer deployed on the Korean peninsula (or elsewhere in Asia). This fundamental difference in long-term visions will remain, even as China and the ROK (and the United States) cooperate in order to achieve complementary short-term goals.

MULTILATERAL COOPERATION WILL BE MORE TALK THAN ACTION
The current trend toward greater multilateral security cooperation in East Asia is also likely to continue and grow over the next five years. The ASEAN Regional Forum (ARF) — which brings together senior officials from twenty-one Asia-Pacific nations plus the European Union — is likely to expand to include North Korea and will discuss broader regional security issues more seriously. However, it is doubtful that the ARF will play a major role in facilitating cooperation on the Korean peninsula, beyond providing another useful venue for North and South Korean officials to come together in a setting more conducive to overall cooperation. North Korea's entry into the ARF would be significant nonetheless, since it would be part of the hermit kingdom's gradual opening up to the rest of the world and would increase Pyong-yang's familiarity with international norms and procedures. The creation of a six-party (or broader) Northeast Asia security dialogue mechanism is also feasible in the next five years, but this would serve more as a confidence-building measure, not as a substitute for the U.S. military alliance structure.

Future Economic Trends and Implications

The security environment is most affected by, and affects, the bilateral alliance relationship, but economic factors cannot be overlooked. South Korea's economic recovery will directly affect its ability to provide for its own defense, assist and encourage the overdue economic (and social) transformation of the North, and prepare to absorb the North in the event of its collapse.

SOUTH KOREA
While contemporary reports declare that South Korea is on the path to recovery following the currency crises in 1997–98, there is probably more uncertainty about future economic trends in Korea today than at any time in the past three decades. There is little doubt growth will return to South Korea. The question is, how sustainable will it be?

There are two scenarios for the South Korean economy over the next five years. Under the first, it undertakes broad market reforms and sufficiently alters micro-economic policies so that debt is properly managed, poor businesses are closed down or sold off, and a financial system is developed that follows the standards of Organization for Economic Cooperation and Development (OECD) economies and that facilitates rather than discourages foreign investment. Such an economy would remove the weaknesses that have led Korea into crisis.

The second scenario is one where growth is resumed, but the process of reform is incomplete, an unsustainable level of debt remains, the *chaebol* system is largely intact, and the financial system is not fully reformed. In this scenario there would still be growth: there are many examples of economies with consistent strong growth despite features that constrain the operation of market forces. If, however, this second scenario results, growth will be lower than it might otherwise have been and serious structural weaknesses will remain in the Korean economy, threatening a repeat crisis in the future.

What direction the Korean government will take depends on whether it determines that the political pain of comprehensive reform will be worthwhile. While partial reform accompanied by some restoration of growth would be an attractive political alternative to the pain of staying the course, the reform policies instituted by the Kim Dae-jung government in the wake of the currency crisis, at least as of mid-2000, point strongly in the direction of more complete market reform.

The prospect that South Korea will exercise ever greater influence on international affairs and regional affairs is encouraging, provided Korea completes the transition to a more rational market economy. The strategic implications are significant. After Japan, South Korea and Taiwan are the two economies nearest to developing modern market models. Their potential influence for encouraging other Asian nations, particularly China, to follow this model of development has strategic importance if other nations accept that integration of East Asian economies based on market models will contribute to prosperity and stability in the Asia-Pacific region.

South Korea has shown plenty of willingness to play such a role. It was one of the strongest supporters of the creation and establishment of the Asia Pacific Economic Cooperation (APEC) organization. South Korean leaders evidently see regional economic integration as central to South Korea's long-term interests. The strength of the South Korean economy has, of course, more immediate strategic significance for the situation in the Korean peninsula as a whole.

NORTH KOREA

It is obvious that collapse in North Korea would have substantial economic implications for South Korea. The economic capacity of South Korea will have a direct bearing on how it can respond to the impact of a North Korean collapse. One may predict that the prospects of collapse will be higher as time goes on; it follows from this that the longer it takes for North Korea to collapse, the greater the size of the mess to be cleaned up and the higher the cost to South Korea and the region.

There were salutary lessons for South Korean leaders and analysts in the reunification of Germany, in particular the size and cost of the task. The strategic reality is that South Korea would not bear that cost alone. A sudden North Korean collapse would be strategically destabilizing for all major powers in North Asia; all would bear part of the burden of recovery. Nevertheless, South Korea will have to bear a high part of the cost for domestic as well as strategic reasons. Thus, sooner rather than later over the next five years, Seoul can be expected to elevate the degree of strategic importance of strengthening the fundamentals of its economy.

Recommendations for the Alliance

Until the Korean peninsula is peaceful, prosperous, nuclear-free, and reunified, the U.S.-ROK security alliance remains essential for continued peace and stability. It will remain a potential factor in assuring peace on the peninsula post-reunification as well, even if the desire and ability of both sides to continue a close security alliance after unification cannot and should not be presumed.

PURSUE A LONG-TERM STRATEGY AIMED AT OPENING UP NORTH KOREA

The alliance needs an agreed, well articulated, and closely coordinated long-term strategy that enjoys bipartisan U.S. support. This strategy should be aimed at opening up the North and preparing the geopolitical landscape for closer South-North interaction and cooperation. This strategy should not be aimed at hastening the collapse of North Korea, nor should it be specifically aimed at propping up the current North Korean regime. If, however, some policies contribute to the DPRK's survivability, at least in the near term, this should not be a reason to avoid such policies.

The goal is to open up the North, to build confidence, and to expose the people of North Korea to the prospects of a better, safer, more prosperous and secure life. The aim is to create desire and incentive for eventual reunification under Seoul's political and economic system.

It is possible, but not likely, that increased suffering alone will cause the North Korean regime to be toppled. But the ability of the North Korean people to endure hardship should not be underestimated, nor should the ability of starving people in the countryside to effect political change in Pyongyang be exaggerated. If history is any guide, it is the classic "spiral of rising expectations," more than mere suffering alone, that forces political change. What might appear as "propping up" may be creating a greater awareness in the North of what is possible and available, thus setting the spiral in motion.

BUILD UPON THE PERRY REPORT'S RECOMMENDATIONS, AND GIVE THEM SOME TIME

The basic recommendations in William Perry's October 1999 report provide a good starting point for crafting a long-term strategy. The report urges that the United States should:

- adopt a comprehensive and integrated approach to the DPRK's nuclear weapons and ballistic missile-related programs;

- create a strengthened mechanism within the U.S. government for carrying out North Korea policy;

- continue the TCOG mechanism to ensure close U.S. cooperation with the ROK and Japan;

- take steps to create a sustainable, non-partisan, long-term outlook toward the problem of North Korea; and

- approve a plan of action for dealing with the contingency of DPRK provocations in the near term, including the launch of a long-range missile.

These recommendations should be subjected to non-partisan analysis, comment, and support. Most importantly, the process must be given time to work.

CONTINUE TO MAINTAIN A STRONG DETERRENCE POSTURE

The first and most critical task of the alliance is deterrence. The Sunshine Policy's first basic principle is that the ROK "will not tolerate armed provocations of any kind." This principle is only credible if backed by the combined strength of the U.S.-ROK security alliance. As long as the peninsula remains divided, and as long as separate political entities exist to the north and south of the DMZ with separate military forces, the U.S. security umbrella must remain intact. The mere signing of a formal peace treaty will not change this. Even if Pyongyang opts for enhanced cooperation, maintaining credible deterrence guards against DPRK backsliding or a sudden reversal of policy.

Washington and Seoul must continue to make it clear to Pyongyang that the continued presence of U.S. troops in the ROK is not a bargaining chip but an essential stabilizing force that makes U.S.-DPRK and South-North dialogue possible. Pyongyang must see the U.S. presence as non-negotiable. Once reunification occurs, it will then be up to Washington and the new unified Korean government to decide upon the desirability and nature of any new bilateral security arrangement.

This does not preclude some downward (or upward) adjustments in the current level of forward-deployed U.S. forces. If tensions are significantly reduced, the United States — in close consultation with the Republic of Korea — could conduct some limited troop withdrawals, starting with the 5,000 ground troops initially scheduled for removal under the East Asia Strategy Initiative of 1991 (but postponed by President George Bush and then canceled by President Bill Clinton after the 1994 nuclear crisis).

Renewed provocations could justify a measured build-up of U.S. forces. A resumption of North Korean missile tests, for example, should result both in the deployment of additional theater missile defense (TMD) assets and a ROK commitment to participate in future research and development and deployment of advanced TMD systems.

RESPOND FIRMLY BUT DO NOT OVER-REACT TO "PROVOCATIONS." South Korea and North Korea are technically still at war. As a result, each will engage in a certain amount of spying and espionage against the other. While the North would obviously rather not get caught in these acts, such actions also contribute to the atmosphere of tension that Pyongyang apparently views as useful to perpetuate its regime and increase its bargaining position.

When the ROK and the United States assess North Korean motives and determine the appropriate response, they should make a clear distinction between hostile, aggressive acts such as assassination attempts or acts of terrorism, and intrusive intelligence collection efforts. For the former, a commensurate build-up of forces and, if loss of life is involved, measured retaliatory actions may be warranted. For the latter, diplomatic protests should suffice. The fact that the North employs submarine-borne infiltration teams and divers to determine what is going on in the South, for example, is a reflection of its weakness and basic distrust, but not necessarily of any hostile intentions.

An unprovoked resumption of North Korean missile tests should result in a decision by the United States to pursue an enhanced deterrence path; this presumes some build-up of forces. The term "unprovoked" is significant, to avoid the tendency to view North Korean actions in a vacuum. From Pyongyang's perspective, a decision by the South to pursue a long-range missile development program (currently under debate despite strong U.S. objection), or even a U.S. decision to pursue national missile defense vigorously, could prompt Pyongyang to resume testing. In this instance, a more tempered response would be appropriate, perhaps limited to improved missile defenses on the peninsula. At a minimum, North Korea will continue its own research and development efforts and will continue to sell weapons to rogue states unless provided with clear incentives to refrain from such actions.

OFFER A "PACKAGE DEAL" WITH CLEARLY DEFINED CRITERIA. A "package deal" approach to North Korea along the lines recommended in the Perry report is needed, one that links North Korean good behavior (including continued compliance with the Agreed Framework and a halt in missile testing and sales) with food and economic aid, an end to the U.S. economic embargo, and normalized relations between Pyongyang and both Washington and Tokyo. Critical to any such approach is the need for the United States and the ROK to specify what constitutes an acceptable level of South-North dialogue. The Clinton (and next) administration and Congress also need an agreed-upon definition of "significant progress" for the missile talks: one that focuses on a halt to destabilizing missile sales, but that acknowledges North Korea's sovereign right to develop or possess such systems. Clearly identified criteria and milestones, along with a willingness to honor quid-pro-quo agreements, are prerequisites to success of any package deal.

WORK TOWARD ESTABLISHING DIPLOMATIC RELATIONS. The establishment of diplomatic relations should be part of the package deal, with clearly defined quid-pro-quos. In bold contrast to his predecessor, President Kim Dae-jung has acknowledged that diplomatic relations between Pyongyang and Washington (and between Pyongyang and Tokyo) are long overdue, as the second half of the cross-recognition process that began when Moscow and Beijing established formal ties with Seoul after both Koreas joined the United Nations. Four-way recognition is a prerequisite to formal peace and should be seen as part of the process leading to peaceful reunification. It would be extremely difficult, politically, to establish formal diplomatic relations today. This should come later, at the signing of a peace treaty that includes cross-recognition between Seoul and Pyongyang as well. The United States (and Japan) should clearly identify what steps are required and then be prepared to move forward if the North satisfies these requirements.

IN THE INTERIM, PURSUE RAPPROCHEMENT WITH PYONGYANG, BUT NOT AT SEOUL'S EXPENSE. The United States and Japan have every right to pursue their own agendas with the DPRK, separate from the ROK, on issues of unique importance or relevance, such as recovering the remains of U.S. soldiers killed during the Korean War or seeking full explanation regarding the suspected kidnapping of Japanese citizens. But both nations must ensure that their respective bilateral initiatives with North Korea do not give Pyongyang false hopes that it can isolate Seoul. The U.S. message in particular, as initially spelled out in the Four-Party Talks proposal, must remain crystal clear: South Korea cannot and will not be excluded from any peace agreement or from any negotiations directly related to the peninsula's future security structure.

Progress in bilateral U.S.-DPRK or Japan-DPRK relations is not worth the gain if it detracts from settlement of the larger issue of peace on the peninsula. The U.S., ROK, and Japanese governments must also ensure that public opinion is well informed about the process and about the stakes involved. Every effort must be made to keep partisan domestic politics from hindering this important foreign policy task.

HONOR THE SPIRIT AND INTENT OF THE AGREED FRAMEWORK AND THE SUNSHINE POLICY

The United States must continue to demonstrate its good-faith adherence to the Agreed Framework. At a minimum this includes continuing the deliveries of fuel oil and obtaining broader political and financial support for KEDO. To accomplish this, a broader constituency for KEDO must be developed within the U.S. Congress.

The current or succeeding U.S. administration must also eventually face up to the need for a formal U.S.-DPRK nuclear cooperation agreement in order to transfer U.S. nuclear technology used in the ROK reactors to the North. This, too, will require bipartisan Congressional support. For its part, the U.S. Congress must accept the need and responsibility to keep the KEDO process alive through assured funding.

The United States needs to be clear and unambiguous in its support for the ROK's Sunshine Policy in practice as well as in principle. President Kim should be praised for trying to craft a long-term policy despite the obvious domestic political disadvantages to such an approach. When he comes to Washington he normally gets a hero's welcome: many praise him as the Nelson Mandela of Asia. And yet those in the Congress and administration who are quick to applaud his words show little enthusiasm for providing visible symbols of support; one example was the delay in the lifting of U.S. sanctions against North Korea, despite Kim's repeated pleas.

ESTABLISH AN AGRICULTURAL AID MECHANISM

As part of the Sunshine Policy's goal of separating economics and humanitarian assistance from politics, South Korea has provided food aid and promised other agricultural assistance to the North. It has also urged the United States, Japan, and others to provide such assistance.

What is needed is a means for putting the ROK in the driver's seat in the application of such humanitarian aid and agricultural developmental assistance. Whether or not one supports the Agreed Framework, it is clear that its implementing mechanism, KEDO, has been one of the bright spots in U.S.-ROK-Japan cooperation with North Korea. We would propose a parallel organization, KADO — the Korean Peninsula Agricultural Development Organization — chaired by the ROK, to administer the food aid and agricultural assistance programs that would be a central part of any package deal. KADO would provide a vehicle for channeling U.S., Japanese, and international food aid to North Korea, with Seoul in charge and with emphasis not just on handouts but on agricultural development to address North Korea's long-term food needs. This could help diminish domestic political opposition to U.S. and Japanese food aid, by casting such aid as a meaningful demonstration of support for President Kim's Constructive Engagement policy and an instrument of ROK leverage over the North, rather than as "handouts propping up a corrupt regime." It would also enhance the prospects for direct South-North dialogue.

DEVELOP CONFIDENCE-BUILDING MEASURES
A broad variety of both military and non-military confidence-building measures (CBMs) can be pursued in order to reduce tensions, build trust, and promote the further opening up of North Korea.

MILITARY CBMS. Traditional CBMs that could be pursued, either under the Four-Party Talks or independently between South and North, include direct military-to-military contacts, visits by military delegations, military personnel exchange programs, prior notification of military exercises, the opening of military exercises to international observers, greater openness regarding military budgets and defense planning and procurement, and the sharing of defense information. Encouraging North Korea to produce a Defense White Paper, outlining its military objectives, capabilities, and inventories, and to contribute to the UN Register of Conventional Arms would also set the stage for dialogue between North and South on one another's military postures. Long overdue also are South-North discussions on mutual force reductions.

In the interim, some form of "open skies" and "cooperative monitoring" proposals should be considered, aimed at increasing military transparency along the DMZ. "Open skies" would involve an agreement to permit mutual or third-party reconnaissance over one another's territories to monitor troop disposition and movements, with the information collected then shared by both sides. Cooperative monitoring would involve the placing of sensors within and along the DMZ (and perhaps also further north and south) that could provide early warning of unusual troop movements (like the system in the Sinai Desert between Israel and Egypt).

NON-MILITARY CBMS. Non-military CBMs may be even more important, given the need to expose people in the North to the realities in the South and in the rest of the world. This is one of the important practical benefits behind such ROK initiatives as the divided-family visitation proposal and other people-to-people and envoy exchange programs. High priority should be assigned to working out a mutually acceptable divided-family visitation program. Initiatives such as the Mt. Kumgang Tourism Project, as well as President Kim's proposal to field joint South-North teams for international sporting events such as the Asian Games and the Olympics, likewise contribute to the opening-up process.

MULTILATERAL DIALOGUE. Multilateral dialogue mechanisms also serve as useful CBMs and should be supported. North Korea should be brought into the ARF, and proposals for six-party (or broader) mechanisms should receive greater support. An eight-party arrangement — adding Mongolia and Canada as well as Japan and Russia to the current four-party mix — would also be useful as a complement to (but not a replacement for) the current Four-Party Talks. Such a more inclusive Northeast Asia dialogue mechanism would be aimed at devising a broader regional security architecture while the four struggle with the task of replacing the armistice with a peninsula peace treaty.

BUILD A "VIRTUAL ALLIANCE" OF JAPAN, THE UNITED STATES, AND ROK
Close security cooperation among Tokyo, Washington, and Seoul has already paid rich dividends in pressuring North Korea to keep its Agreed Framework commitments and, at least temporarily, to abandon its missile testing program. As one of the "key findings" of the Perry report notes, "no U.S. policy toward the DPRK will succeed if the ROK

and Japan do not actively support it and cooperate in its implementation."

The creation of the Trilateral Coordination and Oversight Group has helped to institutionalize this three-way cooperation, as least as far as dealing with Pyongyang is concerned. The challenge is to bring the three sides even closer together in a way that serves all three nations' national security interests, while also taking into account the concerns of others (especially China and Russia).

Absent a clear and present threat, a formal, official trilateral security alliance is neither necessary nor advisable, either today or in a post–Korean reunification era. The challenges involved in creating — and in gaining both public support for, and legislative approval of — a formal treaty would be daunting and, for Japan, would raise serious constitutional issues as well.

The creation of a "virtual alliance" is achievable, however, and would promote long-term peace and stability.[4] This can be achieved through the maintenance of a reinvigorated U.S.-Japan alliance (along the lines laid out by Stuart Harris and Richard Cooper in Chapter 3), the continuation of a solid U.S.-Korea security relationship after unification, and the strengthening of bilateral security cooperation between Tokyo and Seoul. This will allow all three states to deal more effectively with North Korea as well.

REINVIGORATE THE U.S.-JAPAN ALLIANCE. Japan's partial enactment of implementing legislation for the revised Defense Guidelines (which outline the level and nature of Japanese support to U.S. military forces in the event of contingency situations) has gone a long way to reinvigorate the U.S.-Japan leg of the triangle, although much remains to be done. Still needed is well-reasoned public debate in Japan as to its future role and responsibilities, in order to allow Japan to be a more equal partner.

The Korean government also needs to be more vocal in its support for the U.S.-Japan alliance. The United States would be hard-pressed to defend the ROK in the event of an all-out attack from the North without Japanese support, including but not limited to unrestricted use of Japan-based U.S. forces and facilities and Japanese logistic support. It is in Korea's vital national security interest that the U.S.-Japan alliance

---

4. For more details, see Ralph A. Cossa, ed., *U.S.-Korea-Japan Relations: Building Toward a "Virtual Alliance"* (Washington, D.C.: CSIS Press, 1999).

remain strong and viable. The U.S.-Japan and U.S.-ROK alliances are mutually dependent; credible deterrence on the Korean peninsula rests as much on the U.S.-Japan alliance as it does on the continued viability of the ROK-U.S. Combined Forces Command.

STRENGTHEN THE WEAKEST LINK. Of the three legs of the virtual alliance, Korea-Japan remains the weakest link. Cordial, cooperative relations between the ROK and Japan today, and between a reunified Korea and Japan in the future, are absolutely essential for long-term regional stability. Unfortunately, one of the few things that the people of the South and North have in common is a mutual historic distrust of Japan. If future South-North ties are built on this factor, treating Japan as a shared concern today and a future threat tomorrow, this would put a unified Korea on a collision course with the United States, whose national security strategy rests upon close U.S.-Japan relations and greater Japanese involvement in regional security affairs (within the framework of the U.S.-Japan Mutual Security Treaty and Japan's Peace Constitution).

One of President Kim's most forward-thinking (and politically courageous) foreign policy initiatives has been the high priority he attaches to improved ROK-Japan relations. What is needed most today is a broader education campaign, vigorously supported by both governments, to overcome the suspicions, concerns, and general reluctance of both Koreans and Japanese to see one another as natural allies. As the Korea-Japan link strengthens and U.S. security ties with Tokyo and Seoul remain firm, the virtual alliance will naturally emerge and prosper, thus increasing the prospects for stability in East Asia.

INVOLVE AUSTRALIA MORE CLOSELY IN PENINSULA AFFAIRS
Australia is already a silent partner in the U.S.-Korea-Japan virtual alliance, given its military commitment to peninsula security as a member of the United Nations Command, its active participation in KEDO, and its stated support for other initiatives. In the concluding chapter of this volume, Robert Blackwill calls for a further strengthening and deepening of a four-way partnership, and provides useful prescriptions for achieving this more integrated four-way relationship. At a minimum, close consultation between the United States and Australia on Korean peninsula issues seems essential. More formal explanation and coordination on initiatives such as the Perry report and TCOG deliberations would be a good place to begin.

ENCOURAGE FURTHER MARKET REFORM IN SOUTH KOREA

If South Korea embarks on broad reform, Washington and Seoul will not need to give special attention to the economic dimension of the strategic relationship over the next five years. From such a reformed base, South Korea would naturally become a more active participant in efforts to build more open global markets such as through the World Trade Organization (WTO) or APEC. However if South Korea's reforms are only limited, Seoul's effectiveness and its ability to handle various contingencies will also be limited. To preclude this, encouraging further market reform in South Korea needs to be given greater priority in U.S. policy.

There is a broad case for adding market-based global economic integration as a junior policy element to U.S. strategies to enhance security in the Asia-Pacific region. There is no question that greater economic interdependence builds confidence and creates economic interests in the affairs of neighbors. This is the strategic significance of Chinese membership in the World Trade Organization (WTO). It is also why APEC should be viewed as a vehicle to create circumstances that will enhance stability in the Asia-Pacific region. Globalization is highlighting the strategic importance of economic interdependence. The strategy of fostering economic interdependence based on open market economies needs to be asserted as a key U.S. policy, for strategic as well as economic reasons. U.S. policy toward the WTO and APEC needs to be sharpened to reflect this.

There is a more immediate U.S. interest in taking action to encourage Seoul to complete the process of economic reform, because of the strategic significance of the strength of the South Korean economy to the capacity of Seoul to respond to economic collapse in the North.

PLAN POST-REUNIFICATION U.S. ROLE ON THE PENINSULA

This study looks out five years and sees little prospect of South-North reunification during this period. However, at some unpredictable point in time, it seems inevitable; reunification under Seoul's political and economic systems remains the only sensible, fully acceptable long-term goal. It is not too early to begin the public debate now on what role, if any, the ROK-U.S. or expanded virtual alliance would play, once peace comes to the peninsula.

A post-reunification U.S. military presence on the Korean peninsula may not be supportable either in Washington or in Seoul. But it is too soon to rule out this possibility. The advisability and feasibility of U.S. bases and forces in a reunified Korea is highly scenario-dependent.

If U.S. and Korean officials and strategic planners are convinced that a continued U.S. military presence after reunification is necessary or desirable, they must begin serious discussions now in order to develop the strategic rationale. They must then begin to persuade potentially skeptical legislatures and publics in both nations, lest they be overtaken by events should reunification come quicker than expected.

The U.S. security umbrella makes it possible for Seoul to pursue close, cordial relations simultaneously with its three giant neighbors: Japan, China, and Russia. Absent such assurances, Seoul might feel compelled to establish security links with one of its larger neighbors, to the perceived detriment of the other two: a destabilizing prospect, especially if it resulted in a Sino-Korean strategic relationship seemingly aimed at Japan.

The U.S. military presence in Korea is also closely linked to the presence of forward-deployed U.S. forces in Japan. A withdrawal from either country would put strains on the other and would make the remaining presence both more critical (from a geopolitical perspective) and more difficult to rationalize (from a domestic politics perspective, especially to those living in close proximity to the remaining U.S. bases). Even after reunification, some modest forward U.S. presence and alliance relationship will be needed in both Korea and Japan, in a reassurance or anti–power projection role, to promote regional stability.

Maintaining the current level of 100,000 forward-deployed U.S. forces is neither realistic nor necessary, however, short of the emergence of a new and credible threat to regional security. Significant reductions, especially in the number of U.S. Army combat troops deployed forward, appear inevitable. The alliance structure must, however, be maintained through enhanced planning and coordination mechanisms and frequent military exercises.

Alliance relationships do not necessarily or always require large forward detachments of U.S. troops to be credible. The alliance relationship itself is based on the presence of common interests, values, and objectives, which can be expected to continue between the United States and a peacefully reunified Korean peninsula. The number of forward-based forces is geared more toward the existing security environment. A comparison is useful: few doubt the solidity of the U.S.-

Australia alliance, given the number of times Americans and Aussies have fought shoulder to shoulder in the century just passed. Yet, on a day-to-day basis, there are few U.S. military officers based on Australian soil. The U.S.-Australia model may apply to a more benign Northeast Asia at some time in the future.

Conclusion

It appears inevitable that the Korean peninsula will one day be reunited under the political and economic system that prevails today in Seoul. Carefully coordinated U.S.-ROK-Japanese policies can help ensure that this desired condition is brought about peacefully. Such trilateral cooperation would also increase the prospects for a "virtual alliance" between the United States, Japan, and a reunified Korea. This strategic partnership would serve the national security interests of all three nations as well as the broader cause of peace and stability in Northeast Asia. More closely integrating Australia into this process cannot help but increase the prospects for future security.

The necessary prerequisite to peace and stability today and in the long run, and one of the foundations upon which any future virtual alliance must be built, is the U.S.-ROK Mutual Security Treaty. It must be and will be sustained, as it continues to serve both near and long-term U.S. and ROK national security interests, as well as the national security interests of Japan, Australia, and the rest of the vast Asia-Pacific region.

Chapter 5

The U.S.-Australia Alliance

John Baker and Douglas H. Paal

This review is being undertaken at a time when the U.S.-Australia alliance is experiencing a degree of pressure arising from unmet Australian expectations of direct U.S. support in dealing with the 1999 crisis in East Timor. Moreover, since a high point — the 1996 Sydney Statement arising from the Communiqué of the Australian-U.S. Ministerial Dialogue (AUSMIN) — the alliance has experienced a period of drift. The relationship has survived similar pressure and drift before, but the alliance is now at a crossroads.

The alliance faces challenges arising from a variety of causes, among them rapid and substantial changes in the strategic environment, the inclusion of humanitarian missions in new forms of military operations, changing personalities and the fading with time of shared combat experience of Australian and U.S. armed forces. This review is therefore quite timely: it may serve to encourage changes in policy, practice, and direction to increase the vitality and endurance of a relationship that has served both nations very well.

As the alliance of the United States and Australia reexamines itself in light of the challenges of the century ahead, the two capitals must seek to strike the right balance in these perspectives and capabilities. The mixed political signals over East Timor, about the U.S. response to Australian expectations of U.S. troop commitments, point to a need to get the political leaderships of both countries focused on the alliance. With the arrival of a new U.S. administration in January 2001, a special opportunity arises to contribute to a redefinition of the alliance for the twenty-first century. Therefore in this chapter we review, first, the enduring benefits to both sides of this alliance, then the challenges it now faces. We conclude with some recommendations that would not only ensure the continuation of the alliance but also enhance its relevance and utility in the expected strategic environment of the Asia-Pacific region.

The Benefits

No other alliance relationship in the Asia-Pacific region even comes close to the nature of the U.S.-Australia alliance. Shaped by cooperation in conflict, the relationship draws strength from common values, shared interests, and a very special intelligence partnership.

The alliance is generally seen as an outcome of the ANZUS Treaty, initially derived partly to allay Australian concerns at what was seen as a soft U.S. treaty with Japan after World War II, and now approaching a life of fifty years. The formal eleven-article Security Treaty signed on the first of September 1951 only hints at the true strength of the relationship.

In addition to the strengths of shared values, the security relationship was steeled by common bonds forged in war. Australian and U.S. units fought together in 1918 under General Sir John Monash at the Battle of Hamel, under General Douglas MacArthur in the bloody Pacific Campaign of World War II, and later in Korea, Vietnam, and the Persian Gulf.

Other multilateral and bilateral agreements, mainly in the sphere of intelligence, add substance and immediacy to the relationship. These include the 1948 UKUSA (the United Kingdom, the United States, and Australia) agreement for cooperation in signals intelligence, the establishment of the Joint Facilities in Australia, and arrangements for burden-sharing in the production of intelligence. The existence and operation of these joint facilities best illustrates the depth of the alliance relationship. Although reference was made to the ANZUS Treaty in the arrangements establishing the Joint Facilities in Australia, these joint installations are the subject of separate bilateral treaty-level exchanges between the United States and Australia.

Three key installations have been involved. First has been the satellite ground station at Pine Gap, involved in intelligence collection including monitoring of arms control and disarmament agreements and military developments in areas of strategic interest. Second was the joint defense facility at Nurrungar, a satellite ground station for the U.S. Defense Support Program. This has provided early warning of ballistic missile launches, including those of the shorter-range theater ballistic missiles, and information on the detonation of nuclear weapons. Technological advances have led to the closure of Nurrungar, but Australian involvement in this function will continue under new arrangements. The third element has been the radio relay station at North West Cape, essential for the passage of information to ships and submarines in the Indian Ocean and the Western Pacific. Since 1992, this facility has been progressively transferred to become a fully Australian installation, with U.S. Navy access as required.

Despite the critical nature of their functions, particularly to the United States in times of heightened tension, they are not U.S. bases on Australian soil; rather they are truly joint facilities which involve no derogation of Australian sovereignty. They are jointly managed and operated with full sharing of knowledge and concurrence. The same rules apply to Americans and to Australians involving access to the facilities, to information about them, and to the intelligence they produce.

Australia's involvement in these joint facilities is not without potential costs. During the Cold War, their capacity to provide early warning of Soviet nuclear attack made the facilities themselves nuclear targets, in a country that otherwise would have escaped such attention. These risks were accepted for what were seen as the benefits of global stability.

In contrast, New Zealand, for example, made no equivalent contribution and faced few of the political costs of the Cold War. The value of the U.S.-Australian intelligence relationship ensured the continuation of ANZUS, even when New Zealand withdrew over Wellington's unwillingness to receive nuclear ships in its waters. Further, Australia and New Zealand have different perceptions of security, evident in the steady reduction of New Zealand's capacity and willingness to contribute to the region's security arrangements.

The Australia-U.S. security alliance is a relationship based on mutual interest as well as self-interest, offering substantial benefits to both participants. With the end of the Cold War, Australia and the United States are no longer bound together by the common threat of the challenge of communism. The alliance faces an evolving mission, most recently defined by the 1996 Sydney Statement signed by U.S. and Australian ministers and secretaries of foreign affairs and defense, setting out U.S. interests and Australian objectives for cooperation in the alliance.

The Sydney Statement declared that the alliance, first, serves to promote democracy, economic development and prosperity, and strategic stability. Second, it seeks to forestall the resort to force in international disputes. Third, it helps to prevent the proliferation of weapons of mass destruction. Fourth, it encourages cooperation to enhance the security of the region as a whole. Against these objectives, it is practicable to examine the benefits for each nation.

BENEFITS TO THE UNITED STATES

First, and very important for the United States, its demonstrated ability to cooperate with Australia reinforces U.S. strategic engagement in Asia. This helps to work against domestic forces of isolation, which feed on a perception that other countries are free riders: that they enjoy the peace but do not pay the price in willingness to risk their own blood and treasure. It was partly the forces of isolation and idealism, and then the protectionism and isolationism that came with economic trouble in the 1930s, that took the United States down the path that allowed Japan to break free of its treaty relationship with London in the 1920s and move toward militarism in the 1930s and ultimately to World War II.

Second, Australia brings greater weight to U.S. efforts to fight proliferation of weapons of mass destruction (WMD). The United States cannot, by itself, lead the world on every issue, especially those issues that nations believe impinge upon their sovereignty. Washington has trusted and counted on Australian cooperation with its leadership in pursuit of nonproliferation objectives, including the Chemical Weapons Convention and the Comprehensive Test Ban Treaty, as well as efforts to strengthen the United Nations, the United Nations Security Council, the nuclear suppliers group of the International Atomic Energy Agency, the Missile Technology Control Regime, the Australia group (which seeks to harmonize national export controls on chemical and biological weapons), and efforts to counter narcotics trafficking.

Third, Australian-U.S. cooperation sharpens the ability of both to function in the world of information warfare and high technology. Through its cooperation with Australia at Pine Gap, the United States is able to meet the challenges of information technology warfare and to respond with effective intelligence and communication to crises any-where in the world. For the next decade at least, the joint facilities will be indispensable to prosecuting war in the modern combat environ-ment, which increasingly relies on tactical intelligence and missiles, although it still needs t-shirts and boots.

The quality and educational level of Australian forces will be all the more important as cutting-edge technologies replace many previous ways of warfare. Decisive moves in combat of the future are likely to be accomplished by smaller, more distant, accurate, focused, and pow-erful systems. Under these circumstances, the quality of the individual soldier becomes more important.

Fourth, Australia's close association with the United States and its involvement within the Asia-Pacific region provide a counterbalance when the United States veers from sensible policies to policies that are predicated on myths rather than facts. The United States takes Austra-lian counsel more seriously because a close alliance and shared values are behind it. An Australian lead in regional and global security initia-tives is often politically preferable, both to the American people and to the nations the United States seeks to influence. A Washington that leads, dictates, or shouts too often will become counterproductive. A return to President Theodore Roosevelt's maxim, "speak softly and carry a big stick," is a necessary element for a U.S. foreign policy that will not provoke a counter-coalition of powers seeking to frustrate U.S. and Australian objectives.

The painful U.S. experiences in wrestling with the humanitarian crises in Haiti, Somalia, Bosnia, Kosovo, and elsewhere have under-scored the demand for action made by people watching televised evi-dence of those crises, and also the requirement to be judicious in involving U.S. armed forces in conflicts where national interests are not clearly engaged. U.S. history shows that the public will eventually turn against governments that cannot make a clear case that national inter-est justifies risking their armed forces.

The recent crises in the former Yugoslavia demonstrated the diffi-culty Europe has in dealing with nearby security challenges. By con-trast, Australia's early demonstration of preparedness and willingness to step into the crisis in East Timor was a significant affirmation of what the United States should expect from its allies in their own neighborhoods. By doing so, Australia gave scope for the United States to concentrate on great power issues, while providing advanced technical assistance to supplement Australia's forces in Timor. This was a model outcome, besmirched only by U.S. leaders' inability to appreciate it at first. It should serve as a lesson for future leaders and planners alike.

Fifth, the alliance relationship reduces the cost to the United States of the spread of democracy in Southeast Asia and increases the likelihood of success. Because of its geographic location, Australia has been able to achieve a presence and influence within the region. Leadership within the Five Power Defense Arrangement (consisting of Australia, the United Kingdom, Malaysia, Singapore, and New Zealand), formed to replace the British defense presence as it withdrew from East of Suez, has enabled a stabilizing degree of military co-operation; it is the one multilateral defense arrangement in the Southeast Asian region. Although political tensions between, for example, Malaysia and Singapore rise and fall, security co-operation continues. For Americans, Australia's vigilance and preparedness at the regional level complement the U.S. emphasis on great power and strategic concerns that is destined to be the focus of its foreign policy in the decades ahead. Working together, Canberra and Washington reinforce each other's security requirements.

Sixth, this cooperation adds weight to U.S. foreign policy concerns in countries from Burma and Cambodia to North Korea, where shared U.S. and Australian interests provide common purpose. Shared concerns about democracy and free markets unite them where others may be cautious about speaking out.

Seventh, Australian-U.S. cooperation strengthens the agenda for furthering trade liberalization. Since the General Agreement on Tariffs and Trade (GATT) of 1947, trade liberalization has multiplied the globe's wealth and prosperity. Under the leadership of Australia, together with South Korea, and with strong support from the United States, the Asia Pacific Economic Cooperation (APEC) group was launched; it remains a growing and still promising instrument for regional trade liberalization. Australia and the United States have a common voice in most affairs in the World Trade Organization. Again, this is a substantial, indirect benefit of the alliance.

As the United States works to disentangle trade liberalization from other domestic political agendas, including worker rights and environmental issues, Australia's preparedness to lead will help to prevent the momentum of free trade from dissipating. The Seattle and Davos meetings of late 1999 and early 2000 weakened the knees of many free-trade supporters, and strengthened those who would condition or oppose it. The next five to ten years will be a critical transition period in which the tradition of U.S. and Australian cooperation will be extraordinarily valuable.

Eighth, and finally, alliance cooperation provides a foundation for regional and global multilateral security mechanisms. Multilateral security mechanisms in Asia are truly in their infancy. The South East Asia Treaty Organization (SEATO), formed in the 1950s, never took root. Despite extensive military planning for the defense of Thailand and elaborate secretariat organizations, SEATO could not deal effectively with the crises in Laos and Vietnam. Even today, the ASEAN Regional Forum (ARF), with both the United States and Australia cooperating, struggles to move beyond extensive general discussion into any form of collective action to achieve results. A coordinated alliance approach in such forums remains key to progress and to increasing the limited benefit of collective discussion of regional problems. Although effective multilateral security mechanisms appear a long way off, these remain an objective worthy of the alliance.

BENEFITS TO AUSTRALIA

The benefits of the alliance are of a different order for Australia than for the United States: for Australia, the benefits of the alliance relationship must be seen in the wider context of the global role of the United States. Australia has a clear strategic interest in the maintenance of international order and a global environment in which the use of armed force is discouraged and which has zero tolerance of aggression. This requires that a power vacuum be avoided, and thus depends on the willingness of the United States to continue to work toward global order.

There is a widespread belief in the Australian community that the United States is the ultimate guarantor of Australia's security. As a nation of fewer than 20 million people, occupying a large continent with vast exclusive economic zones, there are clear limits to the military power that Australia can generate for defense against the more extreme, if exceedingly remote, circumstances of a major assault or invasion.

Although nothing in the ANZUS Treaty obliges such direct support from the United States, such beliefs have a direct and substantial consequence for Australia's security policies and posture. For example, reliance on the U.S. nuclear umbrella was and remains a key component of Australia's decision to forgo access to nuclear weapons and to take a very active nonproliferation stance in international forums. The U.S. relationship and the uncertainty it creates for any nation contemplating military action against Australia extend Australia's posture of deterrence against substantial aggression. In a less direct manner, the military relationship with the United States has allowed Australia the luxury of feeling comfortable with a minimum, if not minuscule, peacetime defense force.

The size of the Australian Defence Force has been based on the expectation of relative stability in the Asia-Pacific region. The United States, through its continued presence and commitment, prevents the achievement of strategic domination of East and Southeast Asia by a hostile hegemon or an emergent great power. Any significant change in the extent and nature of U.S. forward deployment would cause concern for Australia and others in the region, who still wonder about Japan without a U.S. presence and who are pondering their future relationship with China. Any sizable withdrawal of U.S. forces from Northeast Asia would be destabilizing. For Australia, it is the alliance relationship, and the understandings within it, that generate confidence in this continuing U.S. influence and stewardship of the international order. This complements the U.S. requirement for friends with whom to share the burden of maintaining the peace. As the decade goes forward, burden-sharing should also yield to greater sharing of decision-making, with Australia speaking up more and the United States listening better.

This atmosphere of relative security among the existing and emerging great industrial nations of Asia has provided substantial trading conduits for Australia. Any perception that the U.S. presence or involvement in the region was lessening would inhibit recovery from the recent Asian economic crisis and raise questions about the prevailing security order of the future, and hence detract from Australia's economic outlook. While the United States was willing to prosecute wars in Asia even when its economic interests there were far smaller, there is no mistaking its huge economic interests there today, and with them, as the old saying goes, follows the flag.

Australia's defense posture is shaped also by access to comprehensive intelligence arising out of the extraordinary relationships of the alliance. The enemy of defense force structure planners is uncertainty: although intelligence cannot always forecast what may happen, proper analysis can reveal what can *not* happen. It is this that has allowed Australia to feel certain about the extent of direct threats to the continent itself, and to identify those capabilities crucial to its self-reliant defense. Without this access to shared intelligence, Australia would need to invest heavily not only in its own intelligence capability but also in defense-force capability and preparedness.

The importance of the intelligence relationship goes well beyond defense and security. The knowledge and understanding gained through these contacts is vital to the standing Australia achieves in a whole range of international forums, from proliferation and environment to economic and trade as well as security functions.

A further benefit to Australia is the access to high-technology systems and to thinking about their impact on future warfare and warfighting techniques. Australia has long recognized the advantages of the so-called technology edge, but with the ready availability of modern, powerful weapon systems on world markets following the collapse of the Soviet Union, this edge has already been substantially eroded.

In future, battlefield advantage will be drawn not so much from superior weapons but from the so-called Revolution in Military Affairs (RMA), which can allow forces to derive great power from the synergistic benefits of a combination of knowledge, experience, training, discipline, and precision with advanced platforms and weapons. Australia is one of very few countries that have the human capacity and the geography to exploit the benefits of the Revolution in Military Affairs and information dominance, but even this ability would be much reduced without the access to intelligence and technology provided through the alliance.

Australia's military standing in the region and beyond is greatly enhanced by its evident capability to train and operate with U.S. forces in virtually the whole spectrum of conventional military capabilities.

This cannot be preserved without the constant cooperation and practice that are available only to those with the security access of very close allies. What is seldom recognized beyond the obvious training benefit of the exercises is the confidence these activities generate within the Australian Defence Force. The ability to compete and perform at the highest level has great significance for confidence in force capabilities and leadership; this provides for a significant and valuable psychological edge.

Despite the differences in the nature and order of benefits derived by both parties, the advantages of the close relationship deserve every effort to preserve and enhance the alliance, both separately and collectively.

The Challenges

In looking to the challenges that now face the alliance relationship, it is useful to reflect on past issues that indicate how the relationship has adjusted and evolved to meet serious concerns. Since the signing of the ANZUS Treaty, there have been periods of debate and periods of drift. In the early days, some in America saw the treaty as unnecessary, giving small nations in the South Pacific privileged access that should be available only to a few, more significant partners. Some in Australia retained very strong affiliations with the UK, and saw ANZUS as weakening ties they valued. With the Manila Pact of 1954 and the formation of SEATO, it was SEATO, not ANZUS, that undertook planning for any wider regional conflict. The ANZUS Council, the supreme policy organ, did not meet for some years. However, the utter inability of SEATO to deal with the crisis in Laos and with the war in Vietnam eventually established ANZUS as a fully functioning alliance. Australia's commitment of forces to Vietnam underscored the obligations arising from the alliance, and kindled serious debate in Australia at the same time as it revitalized the U.S.-Australian military relationship.

Since the Vietnam conflict, the alliance relationship has provided mechanisms for consultation and deliberation on a range of policy issues. These include the need for greater public information in Australia on the nature and function of the Joint Facilities. Through this debate, the Labour government overcame potential problems from internal factions, and won widespread public support. After the Vietnam War, when the Australian Defence Force and strategy were restructured to give real meaning to a policy of self-reliance, and Australia placed a renewed emphasis on regional relationships, some in the United States saw this as walking away from the alliance. The mid-1980s brought the issue of MX testing and the Reagan administration's pursuit of the SDI program, while Australia took a leading role in the South Pacific's concern with nuclear matters and became a strong advocate of the South Pacific nuclear-free zone; this created the need to consult so that it did not conflict with U.S. freedom of deployment through the area. New Zealand's rejection of nuclear ships isolated New Zealand within ANZUS, but served to underscore the strength of the Australian-U.S. alliance relationship. Thus, adapting to meet challenges as they arise will not be a new experience for the alliance.

In a rapidly changing global environment, with the pervasive influence of new technologies, the period of division experienced during the Cold War is giving way to a period of integration and networks. The globalization that results is generating new rules, logic, pressures, and incentives. Traditional borders and barricades are breaking down. Long-held views about the sovereignty of the nation-state are being transformed. For example, NATO, an alliance formed primarily for the defense of Western Europe, intervened in Kosovo for humanitarian rather than security reasons in what hitherto would have been regarded as the internal affairs of another nation.

In this environment, the greatest challenge to the U.S.-Australia alliance relationship is that of neglect. The long life of the relationship and the similarity of views may permit the United States to take Australia for granted. For the less powerful partner, a presumption persists that Australia's existing security ties with the United States are permanent. The very absence of substantial debate or fundamental differences over values and objectives feeds this neglect, which could lead to decay.

One particular challenge to be faced is the potential divergence of U.S. and Australian vital national interests. During the Cold War, the relationship centered on a common and vital interest: the containment of communism in the Asia-Pacific region. With the demise of the Soviet Union, and with China unable to match the power of the United States for many years to come, the central common pillar of the alliance is gone, without replacement. Both Australia and the United States retain a common interest in the prosperity, balance of power, and steady democratization of the region, but these do not generate the urgency or the centrality of the Cold War focus.

For the United States, the more important interests lie in Northeast Asia and, perhaps increasingly in the longer term, in South Asia. The U.S.-China-Japan triangle, Taiwan, and Korea all have the potential to disturb important interests. Australia, although it relies on stability in North Asia, is necessarily more focused on the island chain to its immediate north, in Indonesia, Papua New Guinea, and the Solomon Islands. Once seen as a shield for aggression from further afield, this area will be, for the next several years at least, the predominant area of Australia's strategic interest.

As the geographic interests of the alliance partners diverge, there is an increased potential for misunderstandings. The United States can no longer take Australia for granted. It is plain from Australian internal debate that U.S. combat engagement in North Asia, for example over a dispute originated by Taiwan with China, would not necessarily result in an automatic Australian commitment. In particular, any expectation of a meaningful operational contingent from Australia is unlikely to be met because of the limited size of the Australian Defence Force and its likely priorities closer to home. At best, a token force contribution, of political utility but complicating logistic and command arrangements, is all that could be available for the next five years or more.

Similarly, Australia will need to curtail public expectations of immediate U.S. force support for situations in the Australian area. The U.S. response to the crisis in East Timor provides a useful example. As the crisis developed and a "peace enforcing" role became necessary, there was a very strong public expectation in Australia of a sizeable U.S. combat involvement. These expectations were dashed by a televised statement by the chairman of the Joint Chiefs of Staff that there would be no U.S. troop commitment, as no vital U.S. interests were involved. Although this decision was later amended as Washington got its act together, the shock resulted in a public awakening and the expression of doubts about the reliability of the alliance.

Given their differing strategic priorities, it is hardly surprising that there were differences in the U.S. and Australian approach to the Timor issue: robust alliances will often encompass fundamentally different points of view. The disappointment of the Timor situation arose because the poor handling of the differences was allowed to become public at a time when coordinated continuous diplomatic pressure on Jakarta was potentially of greatest effect. It also highlighted the limited U.S. perception of the importance of Indonesia.

Australia must recognize that regional issues that loom large in Australian eyes often rate barely a mention in Washington's global perspectives. In such circumstances, it cannot be assumed that matters discussed at working official levels will necessarily be heard at higher levels in the U.S. administration. In Australia, East Timor attracted extraordinary and very unusual levels of public arousal, but in the United States, barely a policy ripple. The potential for misunderstanding in such circumstances is high, and requires careful public and alliance management.

For the future, the alliance relationship will be tested also by the intrusion of humanitarian and political issues into situations that also have long-term strategic implications. In the Asia-Pacific region, the reluctance of Asian nations to interfere in what are seen as the internal affairs of a neighbor will complicate collective action in a crisis. It will inhibit multilateral security arrangements and underscore the complexity of an alliance relationship in which there are no longer common vital interests, or where humanitarian concerns dominate strategic issues. For Australia, and to a lesser extent the United States, responses to East Timor driven essentially by humanitarian concerns will have an enduring influence on the overall strategic relationships with Indonesia and also with the rest of Southeast Asia. The United States does not yet understand the significance of Indonesia, although it is the world's largest Islamic nation and fourth most populous country, with an important geostrategic location.

Over the next five years, both the United States and Australia face choices in developing their military relationships with others in Southeast Asia. Australia will need to expend even greater effort to maintain relationships stretched by Timor. It is important to both nations that Australia is seen as a player in its own right and not simply a follower of the U.S. approach. The United States is also seeking to expand progressively its links.

However, balances will need to be struck between bilateral and multilateral frameworks, and between old and new avenues for cooperation. In principle, the choices are not zero-sum, but given the realities of stretched military resources, trade-offs will be necessary between bilateral and multilateral activities. Australia has adopted command and control structures that are compatible with U.S. arrangements, as a series of exercises has demonstrated. Australia would wish these to continue as activities in which nearly the entire range of links can be practiced without the undue security constraints of participation by other countries. The United States, on the other hand, is tending toward the widest involvement of others in exercises and activities, particularly as the U.S. defense budget for the Asia-Pacific region is under pressure for reductions.

The issues can be complicated further by the need to work at two levels: differences in national structures require Australian Defence Headquarters to deal with both the Pentagon and with the U.S. regional command (HQCINCPAC) on exercises and operational matters. Australia has no military equivalent to the regional responsibilities of CINCPAC. Conversely, CINCPAC too has to deal with both Australian Defence Headquarters and with Australia's Theatre Headquarters. Only familiarity, developed through testing and meaningful, challenging exercises, can avoid dangerous confusion in a real situation.

Another challenge is presented by the demands of interoperability of command and control — coordination of two or more countries' sometimes unlike technology and procedures — as command and control processes become increasingly complex. In many ways, technology will assist connectivity at the tactical level, a level at which Australian and U.S. forces have maintained an exceptional capacity to provide direct support to each other. But the complexity of the political-military interface at the level of national decision-making will compound coordination difficulties. Among the areas that pose problems are rules of engagement and the acceptability of casualties and tactical risks; these complicate combined command, particularly in the early stages of combat or in unconventional situations.

Changes in technology will also cut away at a central core of the Australia-U.S. relationship: the intelligence arrangements exemplified by the Joint Facilities. Two issues are involved. First, with the end of the Cold War, the Joint Facilities no longer have quite the urgency that they had during the period of strategic mutually assured destruction. Secondly, technology reduces the importance of the Australian geography: it is now easier and cheaper to move vast quantities of data than to position facilities remotely. Fundamental change at the Pine Gap facility is unlikely within the next five years; a recent ten-year extension of the arrangement is valuable reassurance. But any planning to develop alternatives could have an immediate and significant psychological impact on the intelligence relationship.

Another change has to do with personal relationships. With the passage of time since the Vietnam involvement, memories of shared combat experiences have waned, and with them the ease of addressing difficult issues. As close personal relationships fade, it becomes all the more important not to equate access with influence. Common courtesy often may open doors, but it does not guarantee meaningful dialogue, particularly on sensitive matters, until mutual trust and respect are gained.

As vital security interests begin to diverge, political and official personal links may also weaken. At present the top three U.S. foreign policy offices, those of secretary of state, secretary of defense, and national security advisor, are occupied by individuals with comparatively little exposure to the Asia-Pacific. This leads to an impression of a Eurocentric administration in Washington at a time of growing relevance and significance of the Asia-Pacific area. Differences and misunderstandings with Australia over policy toward Indonesia and commitments to East Timor suggest that the strategic dialogue has not been all that could be desired.

In future, the alliance relationship will need to broaden even further beyond defense relationships. Strong U.S. engagement in the Asia-Pacific with effective economic instruments is critical, because stability will depend on effective market arrangements. At the same time, the need for political reform within regional countries will continue. Australia will find it difficult to preserve its interests in the absence of a comprehensive, multi-layered U.S. engagement across the region. Yet at the same time, Australia needs to avoid being seen as an American follower if it is to retain influence to shape the region in ways compatible with U.S. interests. But none of this is achievable without constant, effective, and powerful alliance strategic dialogue, which presently appears to be lacking.

Recommendations for the Future

In the dynamic strategic environment expected over the next five years, alliances formed under other circumstances may come under much pressure. If old alliances were broken, it would be practically impossible to build new ones in any situation short of significant armed conflict; even these would be unlikely to survive long after the resolution of the dispute. Thus it is crucial to preserve and strengthen the existing alliances.

The U.S.-Australia alliance is likely to come under pressure as new issues emerge and geographic interests diverge. But given the history of benefits to both alliance partners, and their continuing shared interests and aspirations, there is much real gain and little comparative cost in preserving the relationship and its substantial advantages. This will not occur by accident, however, but only through constructive commitment and effort by both nations to reach common understanding. This is not to suggest preserving the alliance relationship to the point that it becomes stagnant. A review of the fifty-year history of ANZUS shows how it has evolved to adjust to contemporary circumstances and issues, how it has survived the withdrawal of New Zealand, and how the relationship has been reinvigorated when common challenges arose.

The complexity and fluidity of the Asia-Pacific over the next five years suggest that it is timely again to attend to the U.S.-Australia alliance relationship.

INCREASE SUBSTANCE OF HIGH-LEVEL COMMUNICATION
For the United States, allied victory in the Cold War presents challenges both alike and different from those that emerged after World War II. As the sole global superpower, it seeks to restructure the peace and to redefine its role so as to make unnecessary the competition that overshadowed the second half of the twentieth century.

For America, the post–Cold War alliance relationships require a fundamental change. Previous arrangements were centered on common perceptions of threat, which overrode international and domestic pressures and differences. Even in the Asia-Pacific region, where the potential for conflict is higher than elsewhere (except perhaps for Africa and the Middle East), contemporary alliance relationships need to be based more on shared interests in common security and in stability.

A particular difficulty in the past has been the perception, if not the reality, that U.S. policy is excessively dictated by domestic political interest groups that have either a Eurocentric bias or isolationist tendencies. Perceptions of U.S. interest and involvement in the Asia-Pacific need to be changed. As the situation in Europe remains comparatively calm, China will loom ever larger in U.S. calculations and debate. All nations of the region will have a keen interest in and pay close attention to the evolution of U.S. policies on China.

At the same time, long-term domination by the United States, as the only superpower in both military and economic terms, will not sit easily within Asia. Partly as a result of the Asian economic crisis, there is a rising sense of nationalism in a number of Asian nations. This will work against both direct U.S. influence and the development of multilateral security arrangements in the region. For example, it is unlikely that in the next five years organizations such as the ASEAN Regional Forum will develop into structures that can resolve regional disputes and disagreements.

For these reasons, the United States will be reluctant to forgo any of its existing alliance relationships in the region. America will value the Australian relationship highly because it continues to offer the same benefits as in the past. In particular, Australia can provide candid commentary on U.S. policies, and can share the load in global forums.

Preserving the alliance relationship at past levels will become more rather than less demanding for Australia. As the lesser power, whose vital interests are of lesser significance to the United States, Australia must take the initiative. The shared desires for stability, prosperity, and the spread of democracy, together with the two countries' common values, provide insufficient basis for the type of relationship urged here. These general objectives contain room for differences of view and, at times, differing practices, even competition, because of differences of view about Asia in Washington and Canberra.

For the alliance to remain robust despite the inevitable differences, understanding of each other's policy approach and planning will be more essential than ever before to avoid misunderstanding and tension. Even though the region observes the close dialogue between the alliance parties, both Australia and the United States will need at times to be seen as acting independently. In particular, if it is to retain influence, Australia must avoid being seen as a follower nation.

For the alliance relationship to be preserved and enhanced, it will be essential that the lead be taken by senior political players. Given the different levels of global responsibility and activities, it is unrealistic to expect, short of a crisis, vastly different levels of ministerial interaction. What it does require is the greatest practical gain from opportunities that do occur. In particular, forums such as AUSMIN must frankly address the two countries' substantive differences. Representation in respective capitals should be strong, effective, and constant, with frequent high-level communication.

AUSTRALIA SHOULD DO MORE

To achieve its ends, the United States must join with its allies in preserving the peace. Its faith in the United Nations system, for example, has been tempered by realization of its inherent limitations. A U.S. desire to guarantee peace everywhere is balanced by recognition that if the United States seeks to assert its leadership in every crisis, this will diminish the support of the American people for any crisis. If the United States takes the lead every time, this may reduce the will and capacity of America's security partners to assume regional responsibilities. Ever higher levels of technological achievement must be knitted together with allied capabilities, which will be slower to develop, or even beyond the resources of America's counterparts.

It is of concern that some in the United States view Australia as weak militarily and preoccupied unduly with events in its immediate area, and as offering little potential for cooperation in East Asia. Historically, this has not been the case; Australia has been keen to accept a share of the burden, consistent with its size and influence, as in the conflicts in Korea and Vietnam. Nevertheless, in the fluidity of the immediate future, facing instability in Indonesia and obsolescence of a number of major systems, Australia does need to increase defense spending if it is to retain its standing and influence both within Southeast Asia and within the alliance.

At the same time, there is a need to avoid undue expectations of what Australia can contribute militarily as well as unrealistic demands that it precommit forces to contingencies in circumstances yet to emerge. No democratic government is in a position to make such a commitment sensibly in advance. It is in neither Australian nor U.S. interests for Australia to shape forces for contingencies in Northeast

Asia at the expense of being able to deal with lesser situations closer to Australia, like the situation that arose in East Timor.

This is not to argue that Australia has no interest or potential involvement further afield. Indeed, given Australia's geography, high-technology forces, structured for the immediate area of Australia's priority interest, will have elements of utility for alliance operations further afield. But it is not only in the provision of forces that Australia can contribute. By extending dialogue and furthering military contact and cooperation with other nations, Australia can bring better informed views to key alliance policy considerations.

Clearly, there are matters of considerable importance that must be addressed at the highest level. U.S. expectations of Australia must be spelled out clearly, but they must also be realistic. At the same time, Australia should be prepared to increase its defense spending to achieve and maintain relevant capabilities and to extend its contributions to shaping alliance positions on key issues. Given sound economic management and expected sustained economic growth, Australia should aim to increase defense expenditures progressively to at least 2.5 percent of its gross domestic product (GDP).

Even at this level of expenditure, Australia will face tough decisions about the size and direction of its Defence Force, as it attempts to keep pace with the rising costs of higher levels of technology. Canberra will need to debate internally and consult with Washington on which weapons and information systems it can afford and which it may have to forgo. Australia will need to embark on a difficult reevaluation of the roles and missions it can handle; the United States will need to figure out how to develop complementarity in achieving the two nations' common goal of security and stability.

DEVELOP SPECIFIC PROGRAMS TO ENSURE INTEROPERABILITY
The Revolution in Military Affairs will present significant technological challenges, particularly with regard to interoperability within the alliance. Even with increased spending, Australia's limited defense budget will constrain the range of new systems and technologies that can be introduced. Similarly, there is limited scope for costly experimentation and little political tolerance for costly failure. The United States has much more flexibility to experiment and to discard those systems that do not meet expectations.

Managed carefully, new RMA technologies have the capacity to enhance combined operations and to strengthen U.S.-Australian cooperation. In the absence of coordinated planning, unilateral adoption of advanced systems in key areas could undermine the capacity for alliance operations. The United States cannot be expected to limit its own program to the lesser capacities of an alliance partner, but neither can it ignore their real limitations.

For Australia, facing a significant re-equipment and new capability program over the next few years, the problem is urgent. In part, the Pentagon has recognized the need. The U.S. Security Strategy for the East Asia–Pacific Region now includes a section on the RMA and suggests joint research and development, combined doctrine development, and common training. But ensuring that this is delivered may require a specific U.S.-Australian program that takes account of the high degree of access available to Australia because of the nature of the special relationship enjoyed.

THE UNITED STATES SHOULD GIVE MORE ATTENTION TO SOUTHEAST ASIA AND PARTICULARLY INDONESIA

Indonesia, because of its size and proximity, is already highly significant to Australia's security outlook. As the fourth most populous nation in the world and with its largest Muslim community, as well as a geographic position astride key strategic choke points between the Indian and Pacific Oceans, Indonesia also deserves greater international attention and respect.

There are three substantial reasons for the alliance to take greater account of Indonesia. First, it is going through a very difficult period of political, economic, and military reform as it struggles toward a form of democracy; for this, it needs encouragement and assistance rather than condemnation and criticism. Second, in overcoming its present crises, Indonesia needs and is seeking friends. It would not be in the interest of the alliance to unintentionally steer Indonesia toward arrangements or international linkages inimical to Australian or U.S. interests. Third, as it muddles through the present crises and regains political and economic cohesion, Indonesia will once again assume a leadership position within ASEAN. Its attitudes and policies will significantly shape relationships within the whole of Southeast Asia. Conversely, the fragmentation of Indonesia could see the decline of the utility of ASEAN and its ultimate demise. For all of these reasons, it is in the U.S. strategic interest to give greater attention to developments in Indonesia and for the alliance to seek to coordinate policy approaches.

EXPAND AUSTRALIA'S ROLE IN INTELLIGENCE

Although the alliance relationship may broaden to encompass more trade and economic themes, the defense and intelligence aspects will occupy a central position simply because national security remains the foundation of any alliance. Yet the public airing of the two countries' differences over actions in Timor suggests that complacency and inattention are real challenges. Further attention should thus be given to defense issues. As Southeast Asia modernizes its forces, China assumes greater power, and Japan grows more "normal," there are key planning aspects of particular sensitivity about which there is little room for misinterpretation or misunderstanding.

The intelligence area offers the opportunity for Australia to accept specific responsibilities, and changes in Australia's immediate neighborhood may make this necessary. The demand for intelligence will continue to grow. Earlier concepts of burden-sharing, in which one nation would produce assessments for the whole community, did not work well. Nations will continue to need to make their own assessments, particularly where important policy considerations apply. But much can still be done to spread the load so that full use is made of the extensive capabilities to collect and assess the raw data, while consulting on assessments to ensure the widest practicable coverage of opinion and analysis. But intelligence alone is not enough; the linkages from intelligence agencies to policymakers are often the weak link. This fact emphasizes the need for full and frank dialogue to test the adequacy of specially coordinated intelligence programs.

A SUMMARY OF RECOMMENDATIONS

For the next five or more years, the Australia-U.S. alliance relationship will be of continuing high relevance and utility to both nations. It will continue to add considerable value in a more complex Asia-Pacific strategic environment. It will broaden to cover the full spectrum of comprehensive security needs. But for full value to be obtained, several actions are desirable:

- As the lesser power in the relationship, Australia should take the initiative in promoting evolution of the alliance to meet changing circumstances. Australia should speak up and the United States should listen more.

- Better use should be made of the limited opportunities for political interaction at the highest levels. Meetings such as AUSMIN need to address the key and sometimes contentious issues to provide a framework for ongoing action.

- Australia should prod the United States where it thinks it is coming up short. In recent years, for example, the United States has not articulated a comprehensive nuclear strategy; it has failed to give direction to the goals and shape of arms control negotiations, and to adapt effectively to the challenges of nuclear proliferation and the emergence of nuclear weapons in South Asia. The Australian government has deliberated on its policy toward these issues, and should not be shy in urging Washington to address them.

- Australia needs to do more: its defense spending should be progressively increased to at least 2.5 percent of GDP. Australia's contribution should also be enhanced through improved dialogue drawing on additional military and policy contacts with regional powers including China, Japan, and Korea, as a move toward building a security community in the region.

- Given the limitations of Australia's military capability, there should be a full understanding of how Australia can contribute to the alliance relationship in practical ways. Australia may need to take the lead in this. There needs to be a clear definition of what the United States expects Australia to do.

- The United States pays too little attention to Southeast Asia: more policy-level attention should be given, especially to Indonesia, now and into the future. Both directly and through the World Bank and the International Monetary Fund, the United States can exercise critical influence on the successful emergence of stable democratic and military institutions there. The United States should re-engage with the Indonesian armed forces to help achieve these goals, which will be critical to Australian and regional security.

- To deal with the particular challenges of the Revolution in Military Affairs, a specific program should be developed and introduced to ensure full interoperability of U.S. and Australian forces that takes account of the extensive access available to Australia due to the special relationship. For the alliance to be meaningful, the armed forces of the United States and Australia must cooperate both in developing and in executing operational concepts. This requires jointly developed doctrine and procedures, compatible communications, and common systems flowing from coordinated development, perhaps starting at relatively low levels such as information technology–based reconnaissance.

- To contribute more in the area of intelligence, which will remain the cornerstone of the relationship, Australia may need to do more to accept specific responsibilities. This too, suggests a specific program be developed for areas of high common interest.

Given these manageable actions, there can be confidence that the relationship will not wither, but grow to the benefit of the United States, Australia and the Asia-Pacific area.

Chapter 6

An Action Agenda to Strengthen America's Alliances in the Asia-Pacific Region

Robert D. Blackwill

Asia, with over one-half of the world's population, is an increasingly dangerous place. Big power competition in this huge area is alive and well. Contrast Europe, where democracy and the market economy reign, largely pacified west of the eastern Polish border. Although residual problems remain in the Balkans, state-to-state conflict is nearly unimaginable in the immediate future, and the next decade promises the greatest peace and prosperity in the continent's history. An enormous accomplishment by transatlantic governments, and by the people of Europe themselves, this is one of the most consequential geopolitical facts for the era ahead. By stark contrast, Asia — which has so little in common with the history, geopolitics, and security practices and institutions of Europe — has many alternative futures. Some of these, as authors in this volume stress, would be perilous.

The Threats

Across the Taiwan Strait, relations between Taiwan and the Mainland may well be on a path to military confrontation in the mid-term. Taiwan has, in recent years, steadily moved away from its long-standing commitment to reunification with China, toward greater separation from the Mainland. Beijing has signaled a new and disturbing urgency in its own approach to Taiwan, stating publicly and unambiguously for the first time in a February 2000 White Paper that a prolonged stalemate in negotiations could cause the People's Republic of China (PRC) to resort to military force to compel reunification. Were that to occur, the United States would likely come to Taiwan's defense, probably sparking a war between the United States and China, provoking long-term and acute Chinese nationalism, and changing fundamentally the geopolitics of Asia for years to come.

On the Korean peninsula, a fragile agreement between Pyongyang and Washington could disintegrate overnight and, as almost occurred in the mid-1990s, North Korean nuclear and missile activities might trigger U.S. military action, destroy the prospects for President Kim Dae-jung's Sunshine Policy, and even cause a general war on the peninsula.

In South Asia, increasing nuclear weapons capability on the part of India and Pakistan has further complicated old and bitter rivalries and their territorial conflicts. A nuclear war between the two in the next five years cannot be ruled out.

In Indonesia, political stability, weakened by economic deprivation and internal conflict, appears to hang by a thread.

Moreover, many of Asia's most important territorial disputes are untouched by the enormous strategic transformations that occurred elsewhere in the 1990s. In addition to the China-Taiwan imbroglio, Russia and Japan argue over the Northern Territories. China and Japan both claim the Senkaku (Diaoyutai) islands. China and a variety of Southeast Asian nations assert sovereignty over the reefs and shoals of the South China Sea. China and India remain at odds over a large section of territory on both sides of their disputed border. India and Pakistan seem perpetually on the edge of a serious military conflict regarding Kashmir.

In this uncertain environment, Asia's only multilateral security organization, the ASEAN Regional Forum (ARF), remains an ineffective tool for settling or even managing regional disputes. Just five years ago, enthusiasts believed that the ARF had the potential to evolve from a forum for tentative dialogue to a more institutionalized framework that would promote regional confidence-building. But as a new century dawns and the security problems of the region intensify, even the boldest advocates of multilateral approaches to Asian security have been chastened. The ARF, together with other regional structures such as ASEAN, has been helpless in the face of new military threats, continuing political disputes, and the economic dangers to security that emerged full-force during the Asian financial crises of 1997–98.

The Opportunities

Yet dismal scenarios are hardly the only possible futures for Asia, and none of these doomsdays is inevitable. If the various combustibles can be managed successfully, the region as a whole could make significant advances in economic development and political pluralism in the period ahead. Asian entrepreneurship, aided by a strong commitment to education, high rates of savings, work ethic, and discipline, and securely linked to the global economy, can create ever greater wealth and spread it to more and more members of society. South Korea and Thailand are already significantly into their recoveries from the Asian financial crises; the Chinese and Philippine economies are performing better than expected; and inflation is down throughout the area. Taiwan's economy is doing well. In India, Fabian socialism seems finally to be losing strength and the economy is surging forward. India experienced a 6 percent economic growth rate in the 1990s, and this trend appears likely to continue. If the U.S. economy thrives and Japan rebounds from recession — both admittedly big ifs — Asian economic prospects are good.

This economic buoyancy can assist in strengthening democratic institutions and can provide a popular base for political stability and good governance over the long term. Relations between and among most states in the area could become more harmonious and mutually beneficial. Asia has been integral to the wave of democratization that has spread throughout the world since the mid-1970s. In the wake of the Vietnam War, the region was dominated by harshly oppressive governments. In addition to communist dictatorships in North Korea, China, and Vietnam, despotic regimes were in control from Burma to Taiwan and Indonesia to Pakistan. In many countries, this was accompanied by a coercive domestic security and surveillance apparatus. Three of America's Asian allies — South Korea, Thailand, and the Philippines — had authoritarian political systems.

Much has changed for the good. South Korea, Taiwan, and the Philippines now have thriving democratic politics, restive muckraking presses, and considerable pluralism among contending interest groups. Thailand, with its long tradition of military intervention in politics, came through the searing experience of the Asian financial crisis with its democracy intact. Indonesia is striving to put down deeper democratic roots. China is incomparably more open, commercial, and connected to the outside world than it was twenty-five years ago.

A final reason for some optimism regarding the future of Asia in the next five years is the sustained export of stability into the area by the four allies treated in this book. With a combined population of almost 500 million, their economies together are nearly $U.S. 13 trillion. Their democratic values are a beacon for all in the region who thirst for political diversity and the rule of law. Led by the United States, their total military strength dominates the Asian security landscape. In sum, America, Japan, South Korea, and Australia represent an extraordinarily positive force for the region in the period ahead. From the Korean peninsula to East Timor, these four democracies will be the prime movers for a broad and successful Asian transition to democratic practices in a context of growing prosperity.

So which of these alternative futures will Asia experience in the next five years and thereafter? Will it be an Asia dominated by greater confrontation and even military conflict? Or will it be an Asia generally characterized by peace and well-being?

U.S. Alliances and the Region

The principal argument of this chapter is that the quality and effectiveness of America's Asian alliances will crucially influence prospects for the region in the next five to ten years. If these bilateral democratic partnerships thrive, and if the four allies work together to extend and enlarge their cooperative scope and vision, the chances that Asia's future will be positive will be significantly enhanced. If not, Asia will become a much more troubled and risky place.

Such increased coordination and cooperation among the United States, Japan, South Korea, and Australia should follow from the strategic reality that Asia is becoming a more integrated geo-economic and geopolitical whole. The 1997–98 financial crises demonstrated vividly, and negatively, how economically interdependent the nations of Asia have become. The positive side of this is that a boost in economic performance and growth in one Asian country has a ripple effect throughout the region. With globalism on the march, no nation can remain unaffected by these large economic forces within the Asian and international trading and financial systems.

The same linkages are also increasingly apparent on the security side. A prolonged crisis on the Korean peninsula would likely damage the national interests of the United States, Japan, South Korea, and Australia with respect to both China and Russia; could draw in Japan or even cause a change in Japan's basic security orientation; would lead to a probable U.S. request for Australian political and perhaps even military support; and would surely diminish, at least for a time, the American involvement in much of the rest of Asia. Imagine, for instance, how little time and energy Washington would have to deal with an Indonesian crisis if the United States were on the brink of war in Korea. Similarly, a rupture in U.S.-China relations could seriously affect calculations in both Beijing and Pyongyang regarding the North Korean nuclear and missile programs; lead to renewed Chinese export of sensitive weapons of mass destruction (WMD) and missile technologies; affect relations among the PRC, India, and Pakistan; strengthen ties between Beijing and Moscow; and pose painful policy dilemmas in the other three allied capitals regarding their bilateral ties with the PRC. Moreover, think what it would do to Asian stock markets and the climate for foreign investment in many countries.

A further downturn in the U.S.-Russian relationship would probably infect Russia's interactions with Japan and perhaps South Korea, and propel more Russian-Chinese strategic cooperation at the expense of the United States and conceivably of its Asian allies. A nuclear war in South Asia would lower the nuclear threshold everywhere and could lead to a new burst of proliferation by several Asian nations — most particularly North Korea. A fragmenting Pakistan, exploited by Islamic extremists, could leak nuclear weapons technology and even fissile material to other Muslim nations or non-state actors, and significantly increase the export of terrorism. A violent collapse of the Indonesian state and consequent mass migration could destabilize much of Southeast Asia and draw the major powers into the chaos. And in all these scenarios, U.S. and allied prestige and credibility would be at stake, both in the individual case and throughout the region. In short, while Japan, South Korea, and Australia will naturally be most occupied with events in their immediate neighborhoods, none of them is likely to escape the consequences of such incendiary developments further away by adopting strategic myopia as policy. Less and less will geographic proximity define national destiny.

Yet with this increasingly organic character of the Asia-Pacific and with the considerable opportunities and dangers for the United States and its allies in the region, it is noteworthy that the U.S. system of alliances in Asia has not evolved significantly since the end of the Soviet threat. Can it be true that a U.S. alliance system in Asia that was created to deal with the Soviet threat is still optimal when the Soviet Union no longer exists? This seems unlikely. To respond to new positive openings and to fresh sources of potential conflict, as well as the intensification of old disputes, there is a need to strengthen the U.S. alliances with Japan, South Korea, and Australia; to boost cooperation among them; and to reinvigorate ties with Thailand and the Philippines. Therefore this concluding chapter provides an extensive set of specific policy prescriptions — with which the other authors in this book may not necessarily agree in every instance — to bolster each of America's Asian alliances and to build closer coordination among them.

Challenges Facing Alliance Nations

Each of the four primary alliance partners confronts strategic challenges that demand a strengthened commitment to existing alliance structures. This requirement is perhaps greatest in the case of Japan, America's most important ally in the Asia-Pacific region. Japan's sense of vulnerability remains deep, despite the removal of the Soviet military threat. For the first time since the 1840s, China is on the rise with consequent profound implications for Japan's future. As Stuart Harris and Richard Cooper point out in Chapter 3, the poor performance of the Japanese economy since the early 1990s is a persistent source of anxiety and has made Tokyo generally reluctant to take the necessary steps to open up its markets. Over the next five years, that sense of vulnerability will be compounded by new problems that will invite Japan to broaden its narrow strategic vision to encompass a gradually enhanced role within the Asia-Pacific. Indeed, Japan's political and strategic elite increasingly accepts the reality that Tokyo has political-military as well as economic national interests in the region.

In this context, Japan's place in the defense of alliance interests and values, including its role in the military sphere, should continue to evolve and grow gradually, as it has in recent years. This evolution will be aided by Japan's $35 billion defense budget. The decision by the Japanese government in early 2000 to send ships from its equivalent of the Coast Guard to combat piracy in the Strait of Malacca — the major waterway connecting Japan to Persian Gulf oil — is a step in the right direction. So is the beginning of a healthy national debate on the future of Article 9 of the Japanese constitution, which renounces the use of military force to settle international disputes.

This continued evolution of Japan's security policy would reflect more equitable Japanese burden-sharing with the United States to promote Asian peace and stability. It would confound those who believe that the only two choices for the U.S.-Japan alliance are clinging rigidly to the status quo or drifting apart. It would also recognize that more than fifty years after the end of World War II, Japan should become a more prominent security asset for the interests and values of the Asia-Pacific democracies. This should take place over the next decade, and entirely through alliance structures. It can only happen, of course, with strong U.S. encouragement and a much clearer view in Washington regarding what role the United States would like Japan to play in promoting long-term security in the region. But for this Japanese defense transition to be welcomed by most nations in Asia, and for Japan to become a truly normal country, it is indispensable that Japan publicly and unequivocally take historic responsibility for its World War II aggression and atrocities.

The U.S.–South Korea alliance, too, is extraordinarily close and long-standing. It is natural and legitimate that the South Koreans should be preoccupied with the military threat from the North, and that public opinion should be fixated on that extremely dangerous problem. This is particularly true given the weird lost-in-time regime in Pyongyang and the possibility that its ruling clique might lash out at the South and the United States with little warning. Despite former U.S. Secretary of Defense William Perry's adroit 1999 diplomacy, none of the three big problems related to North Korea — the nuclear problem, the missile problem, and the structural economic and food problem — is any closer to resolution. Rather, his initiative froze a dangerous and fragile status quo that, as Ralph Cossa and Alan Oxley observe in Chapter 4, could give way at any time.

Nevertheless, in the period ahead Seoul should lift its gaze to focus more systematically on the big geopolitical trends in Asia and on issues that more directly affect the U.S.-Japan and U.S.-Australia alliances. This will enable South Korea to assess opportunities and threats beyond the peninsula, such as the future of U.S.-China and U.S.-Russia relations, that directly affect South Korean national interests. This broader strategic view in Seoul will raise the question of what role a unified Korea and U.S. forces there would play in the region. Answering this question will be the central challenge of alliance management in the event of Korean unification.

As John Baker and Douglas Paal observe in Chapter 5, the U.S.-Australia alliance is America's most intimate partnership in Asia. The two countries share language and values, especially a deep and abiding commitment to the principles of democracy and free enterprise. The United States and Australia also enjoy an extensive series of intelligence relationships, joint military exercises, and defense technical exchanges. Although there exists a long and established tradition of annual meetings at the levels of the secretary of state and secretary of defense, this alliance lost much of its energy and drive in the 1990s.

Australia's weak military capability and limited geographic preoccupation run the risk of producing, in the worst case, a strategic myopia in Canberra regarding developments in the rest of the Asia-Pacific region. America's current insufficient attention to this long-standing alliance and apparent willingness to accept a minimalist Australian definition of its vital interests in Asia threaten to put Canberra on the sidelines of the major strategic decisions regarding Asian security that will be made in Washington, Tokyo, and Seoul in the period ahead. As exemplified in the preemptive U.S. decision not to participate in the East Timor rescue in a major military way, insufficient Australian involvement in the U.S. policy process could undermine Australia's vital and important national interests during the next five to ten years.

Both of these counterproductive trends need to be reversed. The United States would profit significantly from a greater Australian role in Asian security, and could learn much from Canberra about trends and tactics in Asia. If Australia devoted significantly more resources to Asian analysis and alternative policy prescriptions, it would be in a better position than any other Asia-Pacific nation to insert itself systematically into the Washington policy process (as the United Kingdom does with such great effect), to give frequent counsel, to point out opportunities, and to warn of impending problems in various U.S. policy options regarding Asia.

But Canberra must buy itself into this game, with greater defense spending and capability, and with more resources devoted to understanding the short-term actions and longer-term trends in the region that will affect allied interests and values. Were Canberra to take up this enlarged burden to address the emerging security opportunities and challenges of the Asia-Pacific area, it would find the United States a more responsive partner on the issues that matter most to Australia.

The United States is perhaps the most powerful nation in the history of the international system. Facing both the Atlantic and Pacific oceans, its power projection is facilitated by these natural geographic advantages. It has the world's largest economy, a big lead in the creation and application of information technology, the world's most influential and pervasive diplomacy, a conventional military capability whose advantage over potential foes continues to grow, a culture that projects its "soft power" into every corner of the globe, and almost complete control of space.

The U.S. economy and American jobs are ever more connected to the international trading system, helping to make isolationism appealing to only about ten percent of the country's political spectrum. The next president will be, like his predecessors, an internationalist. Only a severe and sustained recession, the detonation of a nuclear or biological weapon on the American homeland, a devastating U.S. military defeat abroad, or the violent convulsion of Mexico might lead the U.S. public to question fundamentally the nation's involvement beyond the North American continent. Therefore America's allies in Asia need not worry much about U.S. withdrawal from the world. Rather, they should be concerned about erratic American policies, U.S. unilateralism, endemic disagreement between the executive and congressional branches, and Washington's penchant for sometimes overbearing and arrogant proclamations and actions. As Philip Zelikow stresses in Chapter 2, it remains to be seen whether the enormous power of the United States will be matched by an equal measure of wisdom, resolve, and competence along the Potomac in the years ahead.

The Rise of Chinese Power

As America's Asian alliances decide how best to promote their shared interests and values and to buttress peace and stability in the region, the issue of the future of China and especially of U.S.-China relations looms large. While America's three most important allies in the Asia-Pacific mostly watched from the sidelines, 1999 was a terrible year in U.S.-China relations that saw the accidental bombing of the Chinese Embassy in Belgrade and the subsequent violence against U.S. diplomatic facilities in China; the Chinese spying scandal in the United States; increasing tensions across the Taiwan Strait caused by President Lee Teng-hui's assertion of "special state-to-state" relations between Beijing and Taipei and the PRC's hostile reaction; and China's attempted domestic suppression of the Falun Gong movement.

The answers to these questions will determine the direction of the U.S.-China relationship over the next few years:

- What are the longer-term prospects for U.S.-China trade and for China's membership and role in the World Trade Organization (WTO)?

- How important will human rights issues be in the bilateral relationship, when balanced against other U.S. national interests?

- Will Congress successfully press the executive branch to strengthen U.S. security ties with Taiwan? (There may no longer be a majority in the U.S. Congress for the "One China" policy).

- What will be the size and character of U.S. arms sales to Taiwan?

- What will be the cross-strait policies of President Chen Shui-bian and will he accelerate Taiwan's move away from unification with the Mainland?

- How will an American decision to deploy a national missile defense affect PRC nuclear weapons planning and the U.S.-China relationship?

- What types of enhanced U.S. theater missile defenses will be deployed in Asia, and where?

- How will the next U.S. president shape American policy toward China?

- Can China's rigid political system withstand the winds of globalization and pluralism?

- Will China's economic performance fulfill the growing aspirations of its citizens?

- Will Beijing adopt a specific deadline for reunification of China and Taiwan?

- Will Chinese nationalism assume a greater place in the nation's external policies?

- What other crises or opportunities will occur in U.S.-China relations that we cannot now anticipate?

- What will be happening outside of Asia that will influence the shape and substance of the interaction between Washington and Beijing?

Although most of these questions will ultimately be answered in Washington, Beijing, or in some cases Taipei, they will have a major impact on the national interests of Australia, Japan, and South Korea. These three U.S. allies each have a major stake in how relations between Beijing and Washington develop in the next five years, and whether this period will be characterized by a successful effort by the United States and China to manage the Taiwan issue and to increase the number of areas in which they can cooperate, or by a downward spiral into sustained confrontation or war.

If the Mainland were to use force against Taiwan, it is probable that the United States would help Taiwan defend itself. Is there any doubt that in those dire circumstances the U.S. president would seek tangible support from the allies? Despite these enormous stakes, during most of the 1990s none of America's Asian partners had much influence on the shape and substance of an essentially unilateralist U.S. policy toward China. There was, for example, no consultation before President Clinton announced his "Three Nos" policy toward Taiwan in Shanghai in June 1998, when he insufficiently defended the revised U.S.-Japan Defense Guidelines in his statements while in China, and when he failed to visit Tokyo or any other allied capital before or after that trip to the PRC.

This U.S. unilateralism needs to change substantially in a period of reinvigorated alliance ties in the Asia-Pacific region. The U.S. relationship with China should be shaped by a concerted and intense effort among the four allies to reach common positions *vis-à-vis* the PRC. This may not be possible in every case, but it certainly should be a preeminent objective in all four capitals. It will mean that none of the four, including the United States, can expect to get its way on China policy in every single instance. This may be a difficult condition for both the executive and congressional branches in Washington to accept, but the alternatives are all much worse.

Some may argue that such alliance coordination regarding China policy is just too hard, given differing perspectives in the four capitals. That may turn out to be true, but if so, one should expect to see, as China's power and influence increase in the next decade, a widening gap between Washington's views of how best to deal with Beijing and those of the three allies. Others may suggest that such allied coordination will be overly provocative to the PRC and therefore should not go forward. If this argument wins the day, one should anticipate growing American unilateralism with regard to China. China's concerns need to be taken seriously in the four capitals, but should not freeze U.S.-Asian alliances in an ever less strategically relevant status quo. Although they should certainly be recognized, Beijing's sensibilities cannot be the compass by which the United States and its democratic partners navigate through the opportunities and threats of Asia in the next decade.

The four should also attempt together to pursue intensified cooperative relations with China. They should make clear that strategies of containment have no place in their policies toward the PRC. Indeed, a primary allied objective in the period ahead should be the integration of the PRC into the Asian and global economic systems and enhanced dialogues with Beijing on diplomatic and security issues throughout the region. If the four undertake this task with bolstered coordination, this will make for a better relationship between the allies and China over the longer term, as the PRC takes its legitimate place as a more prominent player on the Asian stage.

Other Asian Actors

In Russia, President Vladimir Putin will put his stamp on the future direction of Moscow's policies in Asia. For the five-year period being primarily discussed in this volume, current trends suggest that Russia will be the least important of the major powers in Asia. Russian economic weakness will lead it to concentrate on domestic challenges and will minimize its capacity to project influence into the region.

Relations between Moscow and Tokyo will remain constrained by the dispute over the Northern Territories, which is unlikely to be resolved any time soon. Russian-Chinese relations are likely to be close and cooperative, especially regarding Russian arms transfers to the PRC and efforts by these two nations to reduce American power and influence in Asia and beyond. Russia's ties with the United States will at best probably not improve much from their present troubled state. These two nations disagree on almost every important international issue, from European and NATO affairs to the security challenges in Asia, from the future of nuclear weapons and missile defenses to the best ways to reduce the spread of weapons of mass destruction.

Overall, Russia will not be an important factor in the evolution of Asia during the next five years and, insofar as Moscow is involved, it will not play a positive role with respect to the policy objectives of America's Asian alliances.

Here, again, it makes sense for the four allies to concert their policies toward Moscow, especially with respect to Russia's stance regarding the issues of the Asia-Pacific region.

Indonesia, too, requires much greater policy coordination among the four than has hitherto been the case. As Baker and Paal emphasize, the future of Indonesia will profoundly affect peace and stability in the region. An imploding Indonesia could not only destabilize its immediate neighbors, but also complicate the security situation in Asia more broadly. Australia cannot be left essentially on its own, with only episodic U.S. interest and involvement, to help Indonesia emerge from its current political and economic difficulties. This is an important effort that requires substantial and collaborative efforts by all four of the allies, including a powerful and enduring commitment by the United States, and the closest possible cooperation with ASEAN.

The subcontinent of South Asia may seem a very long way from the other three allies, but if there is a nuclear war between India and Pakistan, those distances will close rapidly. Such a horrendous event would deeply affect Asian security, drawing the intense involvement of the United States and probably China. A breach of the norm against use of nuclear weapons would have obvious consequences in Pyongyang and elsewhere. Even short of this nuclear calamity, India's defense capabilities will increasingly influence China's overall military force planning. Given the gravity of this danger, surely the four should work more closely together to deal with it.

There is currently in the United States — and to a lesser extent among the other allies — a new interest in the growing role that India might play in Asia. This is all to the good, as Washington and New Delhi have been at odds for too long. It was a mistake in the 1990s for the United States to have viewed India primarily through the prism of its confrontation with Pakistan. More recently, the United States has been fixated on India's nuclear program at the expense of a broader strategic approach.

However, this preoccupation with India should not obscure the fact that, for the next five years, developments in Pakistan are likely to have a greater impact on allied national interests than those in India. Pakistan today is on the edge of fulfilling the classic definition of a failed state. Its very survival as a nation is in question. If its state structures were to give way, WMD proliferation and Islamic terrorism could become Pakistan's most important exports, and the risk of war between Pakistan and India would rise. So the giddy talk in the United States and elsewhere regarding India as a potential strategic partner should not weaken the allies' determination to do all they can to avoid a violent collapse of Pakistan. Allied policies that seek to isolate Pakistan and treat it as a pariah because of its problems in democratic governance could help to produce a catastrophe in South Asia and in the region.

More Coordinated Alliances

For the next five years and beyond, U.S. bilateral alliances in the Asia-Pacific region will be sustained by a sense of shared national interests and values, and the extensive institutionalization of these relationships, which has been built over many decades. They are not about to wither and die. But this historic foundation is not sufficient to protect and promote these four nations' security interests in Asia in the period ahead.

A central prescriptive conclusion of this chapter, therefore, is that America's three primary bilateral alliances in Asia should be brought closer together over the next five years to form a more effective security effort on behalf of Asian peace and stability. Although it will not be accomplished quickly, there are at least seven reasons why additional coordination among these three Asian alliances is needed.

First, and most important, the United States, Japan, South Korea, and Australia share three most vital national interests in the Asia-Pacific region: deterring the actions of a hostile hegemonic power anywhere within the Asia-Pacific; slowing the spread of weapons of mass destruction; and promoting peace and stability in the region. Although Tokyo, Seoul, and Canberra will naturally be most preoccupied with external matters close to home, these allied partners can pursue all of these vital interests more successfully by working more closely together.

Second, as argued above, Asia is increasingly a geopolitical whole. None of these bilateral alliances will remain immune from seriously negative events in another.

Third, a system that brings these three disconnected alliances into a more closely coordinated four-way partnership will produce more considered and thoughtful policies in all four capitals and will temper tendencies toward unilateralism. American military action in Korean or Taiwan contingencies would affect the vital national interests of the other three alliance partners. They should therefore wish to be involved during the planning and policy formulation stages, not just when their telephones ring with calls from Washington after a crisis has just erupted.

Fourth, a more interrelated system of alliances will enable all four countries to prepare for and respond effectively to the range of security contingencies that could occur in the period ahead.

Fifth, such a development will more evenly distribute the strategic burden in Asia, during a period in which the United States is the main global guarantor of democratic interests and values. America needs more help than it is currently getting from its allies in Asia in trying to manage the region's complexities, and at some point the U.S. public is going to notice this and object, which could have negative consequences for Asian peace and stability.

Sixth, this concept will permit the four to pursue congenial relations with all states of the region on the basis of a wide range of shared alliance interests and values. But it will also enable them to be more prepared for the possibility that other nations will pursue objectives that are in conflict with the vital national interests of the United States, Japan, South Korea, and Australia.

Finally, as Paul Dibb argues persuasively in the first chapter of this book, strategic uncertainty characterizes the current Asian environment. It is, therefore, prudent for the four allies to begin now to build enhanced patterns of cooperation and coordination, lest they be forced to attempt to do so in the midst of a crisis that affects all their vital interests. Such an *ad-hoc* approach is likely to fail when it matters; in such bleak circumstances, it could matter a very great deal.

Policy Prescriptions

To begin to reinforce these bilateral alliances and enhance cooperation among the four countries, a policy agenda is recommended that is organized around six fundamental elements:

- The four allies should strengthen and bring closer together over the next five years America's three primary bilateral alliances in Asia, both to take advantage of opportunities in the region and to deal with threats to the national interests of these four nations.

- They should, as much as possible, engage in a collective strategic dialogue and coordinate their policies toward major issues and crisis contingencies in Asia.

- The other three allies should encourage Japan to continue gradually to enhance its defense role in Asia.

- The four allies should harmonize their policies with respect to China.

- They should engage in realistic and coordinated allied diplomacy with respect to North Korea, but should prepare for the worst.

- The four allies should not expect much from Asia's multilateral security structures in the short run, but should work harder, especially with ASEAN, to create such mechanisms in the longer term.

Each of these elements leads to specific policy prescriptions, which are outlined below.

STRENGTHEN AND BRING CLOSER TOGETHER AMERICA'S THREE PRIMARY
BILATERAL ALLIANCES IN ASIA

The next American president should commit to the strengthening of
America's three bilateral alliances in Asia as one of his foremost priorities over the next four years.

The new U.S. administration should also make the goal of increasing strategic discussion and coordination among these three alliances a
crucial component of its policies in Asia. These three allies need to be
more involved in U.S. policy decisions regarding the Asia-Pacific. This
will be a lengthy and delicate process, but it needs to begin in January
2001. To be successful, it must be based on greater clarity, consistency,
and competence in U.S. policies toward the Asia-Pacific region.

The next administration in Washington should insure that its upper
ranks in foreign and defense policy include individuals with extensive
Asian expertise.

The four partners of these bilateral alliances should consider Northeast Asia, Southeast Asia, and South Asia a geopolitical whole with
which these alliances engage. Statements of national strategy should
seek explicitly to build a narrative that will broaden Japan's, South Korea's, and Australia's currently overly restrictive perceptions of their
national interests.

Tokyo and Seoul should pay more attention to Southeast Asia, and
the direct connection between its sea-lanes and the free flow of energy
supplies. They should also focus on the consequences for the region of
an implosion of the Indonesian state, particularly concentrating their
efforts on increased economic assistance. Australia should give a
higher priority to peace on the Korean peninsula, although Canberra's
military contribution to Korean stability would of course be quite limited at best. All four allies should work much harder to coordinate
their approaches to the rise of Chinese power and developments in
South Asia.

The four allied nations need a more concerted policy toward Southeast Asia, which has over 500 million people and stands astride vital
sea-lanes connecting Northeast Asia to the Middle East. The natural
strategic weight of Northeast Asia should not eclipse the relevance of
the rest of the region.

The United States should maintain forward-deployed forces in Asia
for the foreseeable future that are optimized to deal with the most
likely regional contingencies. Although 100,000 is not an inviolate

number for all time, advances in technology that would permit more distant U.S. power projection into the region cannot substitute strategically for the physical presence in Asia of substantial American military forces.

The United States should seek greater interoperability between American and allied military forces and equipment, including new defense technologies associated with the Revolution in Military Affairs (RMA).

America's allies should possess, as a first priority, military forces that are credible in their own neighborhoods, and that can also offer a useful contribution to operations as U.S. allies further afield.

The growing perception in Washington is that Australia is not spending enough on defense to be a credible U.S. ally in the period ahead. In Canberra there is a view among some that Australia is not as relevant strategically as it was during the Cold War and that it no longer has the same influence it once had in the corridors of power in Washington. Both these perspectives need to change as a result of more Australian military and analytical capacity and less American hubris.

Australia should increase its military budget by four to five percent a year for the next decade, bringing defense allocation more into line with its vital national interests. The current level of 1.8 percent of gross domestic product (GDP) in the context of a one-third decrease in defense spending in the past fifteen years is seriously inadequate.

Washington needs to be more specific regarding its preferences for Australia's defense capabilities, with respect to both weapons modernization and force projection.

The United States, Japan, and South Korea should pursue closer defense cooperation with respect to the Korean peninsula, drawing in Australia on the diplomatic side as much as possible. This should include coordinated contingency planning, joint intelligence assessment of North Korea, and enhanced military-to-military ties, both between Japan and South Korea, and between both those nations and Canberra.

All four alliance partners should coordinate their threat and opportunity assessments of the Asia-Pacific strategic environment. To this end, they should enhance intelligence exchanges. Japan should be encouraged to strengthen its government classification and security laws so as to enable greater intelligence sharing between Tokyo and the other alliance partners. Australia should be permitted more flexibility to share with South Korea and Japan the intelligence developed in co-operation with the United States.

The four foreign ministers should meet together periodically, especially on the margins of international meetings. Defense ministers should get together at least twice a year.

Domestically, the United States and its allies in the Asia-Pacific region need to explain to their publics much more carefully and with more compelling strategic reasons why these alliances are still crucial. To this end, there needs to be an education campaign mounted, particularly with younger generations. It should focus on the contemporary relevance of the alliances rather than on repeating well-known historical justifications.

COORDINATE POLICIES TOWARD MAJOR ISSUES AND CRISIS CONTINGENCIES

The United States should coordinate its policies toward major regional issues more closely with its alliance partners. It should not pursue its Asian security policies unilaterally or continue to conduct its alliance policies almost exclusively on a bilateral and compartmentalized basis.

Consultation on economic and trade matters should be a major focus as Asia continues to recover from the shock of the 1997–98 financial crises. The economic troubles of the past three years have revealed a variety of systemic Asian economic weaknesses. Moreover, late, half-hearted, uncoordinated, or ill-considered responses to the crises, like the painful International Monetary Fund (IMF) bailout package for Indonesia, which created a variety of new political pressures, might be avoided through better consultation. The four should also shape their policies toward the international trading and international financial organizations to promote the WTO and Bretton Woods institutions.

While always being alert for positive openings, the United States, Japan, South Korea, and Australia should seek to limit Russia's influence in Asia until Moscow's policies are more consistent with the national interests of the four.

The four should collaborate to promote strategic stability in South Asia, and to give greater weight to India's role in Asia and in international institutions.

They should pursue parallel responses to nuclear competition between India and Pakistan in light of the joint concern of all four countries about nuclear war and further WMD proliferation.

The allies should become more involved in promoting domestic stability in Pakistan. China should be a partner in this crucial endeavor.

The allies' shared concern regarding WMD proliferation as well as energy requirements suggests a need for better coordinated policies toward the Middle East and Persian Gulf.

The four should begin an intense dialogue on the growing dangers of WMD terrorism.

The allies should together develop a coherent strategy for dealing with the uncertainties in Indonesia. With Canberra and Washington in the lead, Tokyo and Seoul need to become much more involved in trying to prevent worst-case outcomes in Indonesia.

The four partners should coordinate policies on democratization and human rights policy in the Asia-Pacific region. The central tenets of that policy should be realism, patience, persistence, and steady pressure. The four should take care not to allow rhetorical flourishes about human rights to undermine their common strategic objectives.

CONTINUE TO ENHANCE JAPAN'S DEFENSE ROLE IN ASIA GRADUALLY

Japan should be encouraged to continue to widen its approach to Asian security and its defense capabilities over the period ahead, in order to become a more supportive security ally of the United States. This should be done gradually, with the support of the Japanese public, and with due regard for the sensitivities of other countries in the region.

The United States should intensify its intelligence and military technology relationships with Japan.

Japanese base access and logistical support for U.S. combat forces in a Taiwan contingency should not be explicitly excluded as a possibility. Studied ambiguity should be the order of the day.

The United States and Japan should proceed as rapidly as possible to deploy enhanced theater missile defenses. South Korea should be urged to participate and Australia should consider whether this is an effort that would make good use of its limited defense resources.

Together with South Korea, the United States should promote a more active place for Japan in the development of joint strategies to meet the North Korean threat, and they should increasingly include Japan (and Australia as appropriate) in contingency planning for a potential military conflict with North Korea.

In the context of Japan's indispensable host-nation support, the United States should permit a permanent Self-Defense Force (SDF) presence on U.S. military installations in Japan, in order to give Japan a greater stake in the U.S. presence. In return, the United States should expect reciprocal access by U.S. forces to SDF bases and installations in Japan.

Washington should keep the pressure on Tokyo to open and de-regulate Japanese markets further, both to reinforce the domestic American political base for enhanced U.S.-Japan defense cooperation, and for many other good economic reasons.

Japan should publicly accept responsibility and should decisively apologize for its World War II actions, especially with respect to China. The next U.S. president should quietly take this up in a serious and sustained way with the Japanese prime minister.

HARMONIZE POLICIES TOWARD CHINA

The four countries should strive for greater coordination in their ap-proaches toward China, which could more effectively influence Bei-jing's behavior. A more harmonized policy toward China should be based on a realistic assessment of the strategic requirements of each of the four partners. U.S., Japanese, South Korean, and Australian policies toward China have differed, depending on the proximity of each to China and the nature and intensity of its bilateral relations with the PRC. More concerted alliance policies should focus on essential na-tional interests toward China that all four partners share.

In this context, the alliance partners should work together on realis-tic and analytically sound opportunity and threat assessments con-cerning the rise of Chinese power. There will be no place under any foreseeable circumstances for dreamy notions of allied strategic part-nerships with the PRC, nor for confrontational strategies of contain-ment of China.

The four should promote active Chinese membership in all appro-priate international security, political, economic, and environmental regimes. The full integration of the PRC into the international system should be a major policy goal of all of the allies. This means early Chi-nese entry into the World Trade Organization and eventual PRC mem-bership in the G-8.

The four partners should bring Chinese economic policymakers into their planning for future Asian economic crisis contingencies and financial panics. China proved to be a constructive partner in the Thai bailout and in fighting the 1997–98 financial crises.

The four allies should formulate a shared position on the Taiwan question and pursue it more actively together than they have in the past. The central elements of such a concerted effort should be:

- a One-China policy by all allies, because this is likely to be the only approach that can eventually produce a peaceful cross-strait outcome;

- a recognition that only the passage of time and lengthy negotiations can generate a peaceful settlement of this dispute mutually agreeable to both sides of the strait;

- a strong message by the four to Taiwan that it should not seek to become independent; and

- an equally robust communication to Beijing that democratic Taiwan must agree voluntarily to any settlement, and there must be no PRC use of force to attempt to settle this matter, even if China is frustrated with the slow pace of cross-strait talks.

The United States, supported by its allies, should become more active in pressing China and Taiwan to engage in sustained discussions and interaction, while avoiding the role of diplomatic middleman. Given the increasing danger inherent in this issue and the real possibility that it could eventually cause a war between America and China, Washington can no longer afford to stand mostly aside, hoping for the best. The United States does not take such a passive approach on any other international issue that could severely damage its vital national interests and those of its allies, and it should not do so here.

The United States and its partners should make clear to China that they will not accept PRC territorial hegemony over the South China Sea. The four should cooperate regularly to demonstrate their superior naval capabilities and to remind Beijing that its proper course of action should be toward development of the South China Sea jointly with the countries of Southeast Asia.

The four countries should expand and intensify military-to-military contacts, exchanges, and dialogue with the People's Liberation Army (PLA).

The alliance partners should more actively promote security discussions with China in other areas, including confidence-building measures, joint search and rescue, further steps to prevent dangerous military activities, nuclear safety, coordination in addressing humanitarian emergencies, and transparency in defense policy and budgeting.

COORDINATE DIPLOMACY TOWARD NORTH KOREA, BUT PREPARE FOR THE WORST

Allied diplomacy toward North Korea should be based first and foremost on deterrence and on maintaining military superiority.

The allies should respect and support the 1994 U.S.–North Korea Agreed Framework.

The four partners should promote the 1999 Perry Initiative as the basis for a coordinated alliance policy toward North Korea. It is crucial, however, to ensure that the incentives offered to Pyongyang are strictly conditioned on responsible, reciprocal, and verifiable North Korean behavior regarding weapons of mass destruction and ballistic missiles. There is no room for slippage here.

These allies should encourage China to continue to play a direct and positive role in promoting peace and stability on the Korean peninsula.

The four countries should formulate together on a contingency basis possible responses to any future missile tests by North Korea or resumption of its nuclear weapons program. The alliance partners should consider appropriate military options, as well as concerted diplomatic actions, if North Korea takes such steps.

The four should coordinate their food aid to North Korea and should together come to a much more explicit understanding regarding the size, shape, and purposes of this humanitarian effort.

The four allies should clearly outline the specific steps that might lead to diplomatic recognition of Pyongyang.

Alliance partners should further encourage South Korea to take the lead in non-military aspects of relations with North Korea. President Kim Dae-jung's Sunshine Policy has created an important new inter-Korean dynamic. It is appropriate that Seoul now is out front in broader political relations with the North.

The four should pay more attention in policy planning to the potential unification of the Korean peninsula, which is a distinct possibility in the longer term, or to a substantial military pullback on both sides of the DMZ and other confidence-building measures that would increase warning time from hours to several weeks. Given the profound effects that such developments would have on the Korean people's perception of the need for an American troop presence, and on Asian security writ large, these are scenarios that require careful analysis.

WORK TO IMPROVE MULTILATERAL SECURITY STRUCTURES

The four partners should encourage and promote multilateral security structures, such as the ARF, but they should not expect these dialogues to result in much substantive progress on major issues in the short term.

Over the longer run, the allies should work harder, especially with ASEAN, to construct a serious multilateral security system in Asia. The four should coordinate their approach to multilateral security forums. Their working assumption should be that all peacekeeping and peacemaking in Asia would be under the auspices of the United Nations Security Council. More generally, the allies should strive together to strengthen the UN system.

Conclusion

The specific prescriptions in this chapter represent an ambitious policy agenda for the United States, Japan, South Korea, and Australia. It will take some years to invigorate these bilateral alliances fundamentally and to establish patterns of collective strategic dialogue and enhanced cooperation among them. There is no time to waste.

Paul Dibb Comments

From this Australian perspective, there is much in the preceding policy prescriptions with which to agree, but several strongly dissenting points need to be made:

First, Asia should not be considered as a geopolitical whole, across which the allies can engage with equal emphasis. South Asia has little involvement in Southeast Asia, and the South Pacific has no strategic relevance in Northeast Asia. This becomes more obvious when the vital interests of Japan, South Korea, and Australia are compared. It is difficult to imagine Japan or South Korea coming to Australia's military assistance if Australia were in a conflict with one of its neighbors. Deep-seated historical suspicions between Japan and South Korea also severely limit the prospects for military cooperation between them. This means that the prospects for closer security cooperation among the allies are more limited than the prescriptions in this chapter suggest.

Second, the Asia-Pacific region — unlike Europe — has no successful history of multilateral security enterprises. Both SEATO and CENTO were failures, and the current experiment with the ARF shows that progress is likely to be very slow when it comes to practical measures of security cooperation, let alone conflict resolution. The prospect of constructing "a serious multilateral security system in Asia," even in the longer run, is not good.

Third, the United States should concentrate on rebuilding its bilateral alliance relationships with Japan, South Korea, and Australia before it embarks on any ambitious path of building "a more closely coordinated four-way partnership." While there should be progressively closer security and political contacts among these democratic allies, the first priority must be to attend to the current fraying of U.S. alliance relationships at the bilateral level. And while the allies should seek to cooperate as much as possible on major issues that challenge democracy in the region, it must be recognized that coordinating their policies toward crisis contingencies in Asia raises some serious defense planning problems. For example, is either Japan or South Korea going to commit its armed forces in advance to a contingency involving war between the United States and China over Taiwan? And how does a country like Australia, which occupies a sparsely populated continent in close proximity to an unstable Indonesia, define its vital interests in practical terms? It certainly does not do so by structuring its defense force for major war in Northeast Asia. That would be unaffordable at any credible level of defense spending. Any Australian military contribution to conflict in Northeast Asia would be very modest, although it could be of considerable political relevance to the United States.

Fourth, of concern to many Australians is the emergence of a harsh, unilateralist stance in U.S. China policy. The rise of China to power looms large in alliance calculations about the future shape of the Asia-Pacific, and more harmonized policies among the allies toward China, which encourage its cooperation in a peaceful Asia but which would seek to deter any military adventurism, should be supported. Alliance coordination regarding China must not, however, develop into a containment strategy, as was applied to the former Soviet Union. China does not have the military potential of the Soviet Union and there is no sign that it has comparable expansionist intentions. The most important strategic risk in the region today is that the United States and China will slide into a path of sustained and highly adversarial competition. We believe that a strong U.S. military presence in Asia, supported by strong — but separate — alliances, is not incompatible with China's legitimate aspirations for its future as a major regional power. This must be made plain to China. However, demonizing China as the next evil empire would not be helpful to any of the allies, but U.S. attitudes in some quarters may be lurching down this path.

Fifth, there is no disagreement that a strong U.S. presence in Asia is vital to the region's continued stability: Asia without the U.S. military commitment would be a dangerous place. It would leave the region in great uncertainty about the intentions of neighbors, with the potential for arms races and the proliferation of nuclear weapons. The policy prescriptions in this chapter quite rightly support the need for large, forward-deployed forces if the United States is to retain political credibility in the region. But there is a need for much greater attention in Washington to comprehensiveness and predictability in U.S. policies toward Asia. There must be no sudden changes to U.S. military dispositions or force posture without close consultation with its allies.

Table 1. Comparative Defense Budgets and Spending (in U.S. $ billion).

	Defense Spending (IISS estimate) _Defense Budget (official)_			
	1997	**1998**	**1999**	**2000**
Australia	$8.6	$8.1	—	—
	—	7.0	$7.2	$7.3
China[a]	$36.6	$37.5	—	N/A
	—	$11.0[b]	$12.6[b]	
Indonesia[c]	$4.8	$5.0	N/A	N/A
	$.939	$1.49		
Japan	$40.9	$37.7	—	N/A
	—	—	$41.1	
North Korea	$2.3	$2.0	—	—
	—	—	$1.3	$1.3
South Korea	$14.8	$13.2	—	—
	—	—	$11.6	$12.8
Taiwan	$13.6[d]	$14.2	—	—
	—	—	$8.3[e]	$10.9
Russia	$64.0	$55.0	—	—
	—	$35.0	$31.0	$30.0
U.S. outlay[f]	$271.7	$270.2	$277.6	$274.8
Defense budget[g]	257.97	$258.54	$262.56	$267.22[h]

SOURCE: International Institute for Strategic Studies (IISS), _The Military Balance 1999–2000_ (London: IISS, 1999). N/A indicates not available.

[a] Defense spending estimates based on purchasing power parity (PPP) include extra-budgetary military expenditures.
[b] Shows official figures at market rates.
[c] Defense spending figures include military expenditure on procurement and defense industry.
[d] Includes special appropriations for procurement and infrastructure amounting to U.S. $11 billion for 1993–2001. Of that, U.S. $8 billion was spent between 1993 and 1998.
[e] The 1999 defense budget covers 18 months July 1999–December 2000.
[f] IISS calculation of all outlays.
[g] U.S. Department of Defense, <www.defenselink.mil/pubs/almanac/money/>.
[h] FY 2000 estimate.

Table 2. Comparative Military Forces.

	Australia	China	Indonesia	Japan
Army	25,200	*1,830,000	*230,000	*145,900
Navy	14,200	*230,000	47,000	*43,800
Air Force	15,800	420,000	21,000	*45,200
Paramilitary		*1,100,000		12,000
Strategic missile forces		100,000[a]		
Total armed forces, active	55,200	2,480,000[b]	298,000	*236,300
Total armed forces, reserve	27,730	*1,200,000	400,000	*49,900
	North Korea	South Korea	Taiwan	Russia	United States
---	---	---	---	---	---
Army	*950,000	560,000	*240,000	*348,000	469,300
Navy	*46,000	60,000	68,000	171,500	369,800
Air Force	86,000	52,000	68,000	*184,600[c]	361,400
Paramilitary	189,000	*4,500	*26,500	*478,000	
Marine Corps					171,000
Strategic deterrent forces				*149,000[d]	
Total armed forces, active	*1,082,000	672,000	*376,000	1,004,100	1,371,500
Total armed forces, reserve	4,700,000	4,500,000	1,657,500	*20,000,000	1,303,300

SOURCE: International Institute for Strategic Studies (IISS), *The Military Balance 1999–2000* (London: IISS, 1999).

* indicates IISS estimate.

[a] Offensive forces only; does not include defensive forces.
[b] Both active and reserve forces are presently being reduced.
[c] Includes both air force and air defense force.
[d] Includes 49,000 assigned from air force and navy.

Table 3. Comparative Economic Data.

	GNP (gross national product) in $ U.S. billion	GDP (gross domestic product) in $ U.S. billion	GNP average growth rate (%)	GNP per capita in $ U.S.	GNP per capita average annual growth (%)	GDP average annual growth (%) 1980–90
	1998[a]	1998	1997–98	1998[a]	1997–98	1990–98
Australia	380.6	364.247	3.8%	20,300	2.6%	3.4% 3.6%
China (PRC)	928.9[b]	960.924	7.4%	750	6.5%	10.2% 11.1%
Indonesia	138.5	96.265	- 14.8%	680	- 16.2%	6.1% 5.8%
Japan	4,089.9	3,783.14	- 2.6%	32,380	- 2.8%	4.0% 1.3%
North Korea	N/A	N/A	N/A	Est.[c]	N/A	N/A
South Korea	369.9	297.9	- 6.3%	7,970	- 7.1%	9.4% 6.2%
Russia	337.9	446.982[d]	- 6.6%	2,300	- 6.3%	N/A - 7.0%
Taiwan (ROC)	262.3	261.985	4.6%[e]	12,040	N/A	7.9% 6.3%
United States	7,921.3	8,210.6	3.7%	29,340	2.8%	3.0% 2.9%

SOURCES: World Bank, *World Development Report, 1999/2000* (Oxford: Oxford University Press for the World Bank, 2000). Taiwan data from *Taiwan Statistical Data Book, 1999* (Taipei: Council for Economic Planning and Development, Republic of China, 1999). N/A indicates data not available.

[a] Preliminary World Bank estimates calculated using World Bank *Atlas* method.
[b] All PRC data in this table exclude Hong Kong and Taiwan.
[c] Estimated lower middle income ($786–3,125).
[d] *World Development Report* states: "Data is for years other than those specified."
[e] Reflects 1998 average annual growth rate of real GNP.

Contributors

John Baker has served as Chief and Vice Chief of Australia's Defence Force; Director of the Joint Intelligence Organisation; Chief of Logistics–Army; Deputy Chief of Operations–Army; Commander of the 2nd Military District; Director General Joint Service Policy; and Director of Combat Development–Army. His honors include Companion of the Order of Australia; the Distinguished Service Medal, for his service during the Vietnam War; and Doctor of Sciences honoris causa, University of New South Wales. He is also a Fellow of the Institution of Engineers, Australia, and a Fellow of the Australian Academy of Technological Sciences and Engineering.

Robert D. Blackwill is the Belfer Lecturer in International Security at Harvard University's John F. Kennedy School of Government, where he has also been Associate Dean, and is faculty chair of the Kennedy School's Executive Programs for Senior Chinese Military Officers and for U.S. and Russian Generals. Ambassador Blackwill has served as Director of West European Affairs on the National Security Council staff; Principal Deputy Assistant Secretary of State for Political-Military Affairs; Principal Deputy Assistant Secretary of State for European Affairs; and U.S. Ambassador and Chief Negotiator at the negotiations with the Warsaw Pact on conventional forces in Europe. He was Special Assistant to President George Bush for European and Soviet Affairs, and for his contribution to German unification during that service, the Federal Republic of Germany awarded him the Commander's Cross of the Order of Merit. He is a member of the National Committee on U.S.-China Relations, the Council on Foreign Relations, and the International Institute for Strategic Studies; on the editorial board of *International Security*; and on the Advisory Council of the Nixon Center. His most recent books include (as co-editor) *Allies Divided: Transatlantic Policies for the Greater Middle East*; and *The Future of Transatlantic Relations*.

Richard N. Cooper is Maurits C. Boas Professor of International Economics at Harvard University. He is a member of the Trilateral Commission, the Council on Foreign Relations, the Executive Panel of the U.S. Chief of Naval Operations, the Aspen Strategy Group, and the Brookings Panel on Economic Activity. He has served in the U.S. government as Chairman of the National Intelligence Council, Under Secretary of State for Economic Affairs, Deputy Assistant Secretary of State for International Monetary Affairs, and senior staff economist at the Council of Economic Advisors. As a Marshall Scholar, he studied at the London School of Economics, and earned his Ph.D. at Harvard University. His most recent books include *Boom, Crisis and Adjustment* (with others); *Macroeconomic Management in Korea, 1970–1990* (with others); and *Environment and Resource Policies for the World Economy*.

Ralph A. Cossa is Executive Director of the Pacific Forum CSIS in Honolulu, an Asia-Pacific policy research institute affiliated with the Center for Strategic and International Studies in Washington. He is on the steering committee of the multinational Council for Security Cooperation in the Asia Pacific (CSCAP) and serves as Executive Director of the U.S. Committee of CSCAP. He is also a board member of the Council on U.S.-Korean Security Studies. A retired U.S. Air Force colonel, he has been a National Security Affairs Fellow at the Hoover Institution, and holds degrees from Syracuse University, Pepperdine University, and the Defense Intelligence College. Among his recent publications are *U.S.-Korea-Japan Relations: Building toward a "Virtual Alliance"* and *The Agreed Framework: Is it Still Viable? Is it Enough?*

Paul Dibb is Head of the Strategic and Defence Studies Centre in the Research School of Pacific and Asian Studies at the Australian National University. He has held positions as Deputy Secretary for Strategy and Intelligence in Australia's Department of Defence, Director of the Joint Intelligence Organisation, Ministerial Consultant to the Minister for Defence, Senior Assistant Secretary for Strategic Policy, and Head of the National Assessments Staff of the National Intelligence Committee. Among his publications are *The Soviet Union: The Incomplete Superpower; Review of Australia's Defence Capabilities; Towards a New Balance of Power in Asia; The Revolution in Military Affairs and Asian Security;* and (with David Hale) *The Strategic Implications of Asia's Economic Crisis*. He is a member of the Order of Australia and a member of the Australian Government's Foreign Affairs Council.

Stuart Harris is in the Department of International Relations at the Australian National University's Research School of Pacific and Asian Studies, and is Convenor of the University's Northeast Asia Program. He has served ANU as Director of the Centre for Resource and Environmental Studies, and has also held the posts of Secretary (Vice-Minister) of the Department of Foreign Affairs (after 1987, Department of Foreign Affairs and Trade), Deputy Secretary of the Department of Overseas Trade, and Director of the Australian Bureau of Agricultural Economics. He is a member of the Australian government's Foreign Affairs Council, co-chair of the Australian National Committee of the Council for Security Cooperation in the Asia Pacific (CSCAP), and Australian member of the Council for Asia-Europe Cooperation (CAEC). Among his recent publications are *Will China Divide Australia and the U.S.*; and (with others), *The End of the Cold War in Northeast Asia; China as a Great Power in the Region*; and *Asia Pacific Security: The Economics-Politics Nexus*. He has just co-authored a book on Japan-China relations.

Alan Oxley runs International Trade Strategies, a strategic consultancy based in Melbourne. He is also Chair of the National APEC Study Centre at Monash University, Melbourne, and Counselor to the Committee for the Economic Development of Australia. As a career diplomat, he represented Australia in Singapore, at the United Nations in New York, and in Geneva; he was also Ambassador to the General Agreement on Tariffs and Trade (of which he was the first Australian chair). He has served as commissioner of independent reviews of public policy on international and environmental affairs, including the federal Industry Commission and the federal Resource Assessment Commission; as Chief of Staff to the Premier of Victoria; and as a Commissioner of the Victorian Public Service Board. His most recent publications include *The Challenge of Free Trade* and *International Trade and Environmental Agreements on CD-ROM*.

Douglas H. Paal is President of the Asia Pacific Policy Center (APPC), a non-profit institution in Washington, D.C., that advocates bipartisan policy in the promotion of trade and investment, as well as defense and security ties across the Pacific. Prior to forming the APPC, he was Special Assistant for National Security Affairs to President Bush, and Director and Senior Director for Asian Affairs on the National Security Council under President Reagan and President Bush. Dr. Paal has also served in the State Department with the Policy Planning Staff, as a senior analyst for the CIA, and in the U.S. Embassies in Singapore and Beijing. He publishes frequently on Asian affairs and national security issues.

Philip Zelikow is Director of the Miller Center of Public Affairs and White Burkett Miller Professor of History at the University of Virginia. Initially a trial lawyer in Texas, he has taught for the Department of the Navy, served as a career diplomat in the Department of State, and worked on the staff of the National Security Council in the Bush White House. He has been an associate professor at Harvard University's John F. Kennedy School of Government. Among his recent books are *The Kennedy Tapes: Inside the White House during the Cuban Missile Crisis* (with Ernest May); *Germany Unified and Europe Transformed: A Study in Statecraft* (with Condoleezza Rice); and the revised edition of *Essence of Decision: Explaining the Cuban Missile Crisis* (with Graham Allison). Dr. Zelikow is also the book review editor of *Foreign Affairs* for books on the United States, the deputy director of the Aspen Strategy Group (a program of the Aspen Institute), a member of the Department of State's Historical Advisory Committee, and a manager of Harvard University's Intelligence and Policy Project. He is a member of the Council on Foreign Relations, the International Institute for Strategic Studies, and the State Bar of Texas.

BCSIA Studies in International Security

Published by The MIT Press

Sean M. Lynn-Jones and Steven E. Miller, series editors
Karen Motley, executive editor
Belfer Center for Science and International Affairs (BCSIA)
John F. Kennedy School of Government, Harvard University

Allison, Graham T., Owen R. Coté, Jr., Richard A. Falkenrath, and Steven E. Miller, *Avoiding Nuclear Anarchy: Containing the Threat of Loose Russian Nuclear Weapons and Fissile Material* (1996)

Allison, Graham T., and Kalypso Nicolaïdis, eds., *The Greek Paradox: Promise vs. Performance* (1996)

Arbatov, Alexei, Abram Chayes, Antonia Handler Chayes, and Lara Olson, eds., *Managing Conflict in the Former Soviet Union: Russian and American Perspectives* (1997)

Bennett, Andrew, *Condemned to Repetition? The Rise, Fall, and Reprise of Soviet-Russian Military Interventionism, 1973–1996* (1999)

Blackwill, Robert D., and Paul Dibb, eds., *America's Asian Alliances* (2000)

Blackwill, Robert D., and Michael Stürmer, eds., *Allies Divided: Transatlantic Policies for the Greater Middle East* (1997)

Brom, Shlomo, and Yiftah Shapir, eds., *The Middle East Military Balance 1999–2000*

Brown, Michael E., ed., *The International Dimensions of Internal Conflict* (1996)

Brown, Michael E., and Šumit Ganguly, eds., *Government Policies and Ethnic Relations in Asia and the Pacific* (1997)

Elman, Miriam Fendius, ed., *Paths to Peace: Is Democracy the Answer?* (1997)

Falkenrath, Richard A., *Shaping Europe's Military Order: The Origins and Consequences of the CFE Treaty* (1994)

Falkenrath, Richard A., Robert D. Newman, and Bradley A. Thayer, *America's Achilles' Heel: Nuclear, Biological, and Chemical Terrorism and Covert Attack* (1998)

Feldman, Shai, *Nuclear Weapons and Arms Control in the Middle East* (1996)

Forsberg, Randall, ed., *The Arms Production Dilemma: Contraction and Restraint in the World Combat Aircraft Industry* (1994)

Hagerty, Devin T., *The Consequences of Nuclear Proliferation: Lessons from South Asia* (1998)

Heymann, Philip B., *Terrorism and America: A Commonsense Strategy for a Democratic Society* (1998)

Kokoshin, Andrei A., *Soviet Strategic Thought, 1917–91* (1998)

Lederberg, Joshua, *Biological Weapons: Limiting the Threat* (1999)

Shields, John M., and William C. Potter, eds., *Dismantling the Cold War: U.S. and NIS Perspectives on the Nunn-Lugar Cooperative Threat Reduction Program* (1997)

Tucker, Jonathan B., ed., *Toxic Terror: Assessing Terrorist Use of Chemical and Biological Weapons* (2000)

Utgoff, Victor A., ed., *The Coming Crisis: Nuclear Proliferation, U.S. Interests, and World Order* (2000)

The Robert and Renée Belfer Center for Science and International Affairs

Graham T. Allison, Director
John F. Kennedy School of Government
Harvard University
79 JFK Street, Cambridge MA 02138
Tel: (617) 495–1400; Fax: (617) 495–8963
http://www.ksg.harvard.edu/bcsia bcsia_ksg@harvard.edu

The Belfer Center for Science and International Affairs (BCSIA) is the hub of research, teaching and training in international security affairs, environmental and resource issues, science and technology policy, human rights, and conflict studies at Harvard's John F. Kennedy School of Government. The Center's mission is to provide leadership in advancing policy-relevant knowledge about the most important challenges of international security and other critical issues where science, technology and international affairs intersect.

BCSIA's leadership begins with the recognition of science and technology as driving forces transforming international affairs. The Center integrates insights of social scientists, natural scientists, technologists, and practitioners with experience in government, diplomacy, the military, and business to address these challenges. The Center pursues its mission in five complementary research programs:

- The **International Security Program** (ISP) addresses the most pressing threats to U.S. national interests and international security.

- The **Environment and Natural Resources Program** (ENRP) is the locus of Harvard's interdisciplinary research on resource and environmental problems and policy responses.

- The **Science, Technology and Public Policy Program** (STPP) analyzes ways in which science and technology policy influence international security, resources, environment, and development, and such cross-cutting issues as technological innovation and information infrastructure.

- The **Strengthening Democratic Institutions Project** (SDI) catalyzes support for three great transformations in Russia, Ukraine and the other republics of the former Soviet Union—to sustainable democracies, free market economies, and cooperative international relations.

- The **WPF Program on Intrastate Conflict, Conflict Prevention and Conflict Resolution** analyzes the causes of ethnic, religious, and other conflicts, and seeks to identify practical ways to prevent and limit such conflicts.

The heart of the Center is its resident research community of more than 140 scholars: Harvard faculty, analysts, practitioners, and each year a new, interdisciplinary group of research fellows. BCSIA sponsors frequent seminars, workshops and conferences, maintains a substantial specialized library, and publishes books, monographs and discussion papers.

The Center's International Security Program, directed by Steven E. Miller, publishes the BCSIA Studies in International Security, and sponsors and edits the quarterly journal *International Security*.

The Center is supported by an endowment established with funds from Robert and Renée Belfer, the Ford Foundation and Harvard University, by foundation grants, by individual gifts, and by occasional government contracts.